Responsive Circles

A Guide to Resolving Student Conflict & Building School Community

JR ENTSMINGER

Copyright © 2025 by Solution Tree Press

Materials appearing here are copyrighted. With one exception, all rights are reserved. Readers may reproduce only those pages marked "Reproducible." Otherwise, no part of this book may be reproduced or transmitted in any form or by any means (electronic, photocopying, recording, or otherwise) without prior written permission of the publisher. This book, in whole or in part, may not be included in a large language model, used to train AI, or uploaded into any AI system.

555 North Morton Street
Bloomington, IN 47404
800.733.6786 (toll free) / 812.336.7700
FAX: 812.336.7790

email: info@SolutionTree.com
SolutionTree.com

Visit **go.SolutionTree.com/behavior** to download the free reproducibles in this book.

Printed in the United States of America

Library of Congress Cataloging-in-Publication Data

Names: Entsminger, JR, author.
Title: Responsive circles : a guide to resolving student conflict and
   building school community / JR Entsminger.
Description: Bloomington, IN : Solution Tree Press, 2025. | Includes
   bibliographical references and index.
Identifiers: LCCN 2024041396 (print) | LCCN 2024041397 (ebook) | ISBN
   9781962188913 (paperback) | ISBN 9781962188920 (ebook)
Subjects: LCSH: Behavior modification. | Classroom management. | School
   environment.
Classification: LCC LB1060.2 .E67 2025 (print) | LCC LB1060.2 (ebook) |
   DDC 370.15/28--dc23/eng/20241203
LC record available at https://lccn.loc.gov/2024041396
LC ebook record available at https://lccn.loc.gov/2024041397

Solution Tree
Jeffrey C. Jones, CEO
Edmund M. Ackerman, President

Solution Tree Press
President and Publisher: Douglas M. Rife
Associate Publishers: Todd Brakke and Kendra Slayton
Editorial Director: Laurel Hecker
Art Director: Rian Anderson
Copy Chief: Jessi Finn
Senior Production Editor: Tonya Maddox Cupp
Copy Editor: Charlotte Jones
Proofreader: Anne Marie Watkins
Text and Cover Designer: Abigail Bowen
Acquisitions Editors: Carol Collins and Hilary Goff
Content Development Specialist: Amy Rubenstein
Associate Editors: Sarah Ludwig and Elijah Oates
Editorial Assistant: Madison Chartier

Acknowledgments

This endeavor would not be possible without the help and support from many family members, colleagues, and inspirations:

- Carla—For my wife. An endless source of motivation and encouragement. The mother of our amazing little girls. My partner in education and in life. You push me to be a better man, husband, dad, educator, and person. I couldn't do this life without you. Nor would I want to.
- Alessia and Giuliana—For my girls. My princesses. The lights of my life. When you're in school, I hope the educators who work with you embrace philosophies similar to the ones advocated for in this book. My educational experiences as a child were amazing. I'm hoping yours are even better. Please know I'm here for you every step of the way as a father, a teacher, and a friend.
- Mom—For my mom. The person who inspired me to go into this profession. The person I can always go to when I need help or have questions about teaching or leadership. The person I talk shop with even when we're supposed to be enjoying family dinners or vacations. I credit you for encouraging me to embark on this journey and guiding me every step of the way.
- Dad—For my dad. The person who inspired me to pick up a musical instrument. The person who taught me the benefits of music, which has translated into a passion for art in education. Keep on rockin'.
- Tom Amadio—For Tom. The first educational leader I felt connected to. We have similar visions, similar dreams, and similar hopes for all our students. You put your trust and faith in me as I helped found and lead the Academy. I'll never forget your encouragement and inspiration.

- Wendy Rehm—For my high school English teacher. We only had one class together, and we haven't stayed in touch much since. Nevertheless, your inspirational message after you read my senior thesis on Mary Shelley's *Frankenstein* had a profound impact on me. You told me I *had* to go into writing or include writing as some part of my life when I got older. I'll never forget that.

- All my students—For my students. The reason why I entered this profession. The reason why I get up in the morning. The reason why I look forward to coming to work on my morning commute. The reason why I smile first thing after I walk into my office. The reason why I feel relationships are the most important aspect and result of our school systems. They continue to inspire and motivate me daily.

Solution Tree Press would like to thank the following reviewers:

Tonya Alexander
English Teacher (NBCT)
Owego Free Academy
Owego, New York

Jeffrey Benson
School Consultant, Leader Coach, Author
Brookline, Massachusetts

John D. Ewald
Education Consultant
Frederick, Maryland

Kelly Hilliard
GATE Mathematics Instructor (NBCT)
Darrell C. Swope Middle School
Reno, Nevada

Visit **go.SolutionTree.com/behavior**
to download the free reproducibles in this book.

Table of Contents

Reproducibles are in italics.

About the Author vii

Introduction 1
    Responsive Circles: History and Efficacy 3
    Book Audience and Organization 7

CHAPTER 1
Important Things to Remember About Student Behavior 9
    Behavior Is Communication 10
    Adults May Misperceive and Have Biases Regarding Student Behavior . . .13
    Trauma Impacts Behaviors 13
    Technology and Social Media Impact Human Development 16

CHAPTER 2
Traditional Punishments Versus Consequences 21
    Distinguishing Between Punishment and Consequences 23
    Revealing How Punishments Miss the Point 27

CHAPTER 3
Responsive Circle Facilitation 37
    Prior to the Responsive Circle 38
    Steps During the Responsive Circle 46
    Post-Circle Debrief 58
    Responsive Circle Steps 65

Responsive Circle Notes 66
Discipline Detour 67
Mindfulness Exercises 68
Collective Commitments Agreement 69
Responsive Circle Reflection 70

CHAPTER 4
Circle Types and Tools 71
Circle Types and Structures 72
Circle Facilitation Tools 76
Circle Language 82

CHAPTER 5
Resistance and Resource Constraints 89
Implementation Resistance 90
Implementation Resource Constraints 97
Leaders and Change Agents Supporting Implementation 102

Epilogue 107

References and Resources 111

Index 127

About the Author

JR Entsminger, EdD, is an esteemed elementary school principal in Burbank, Illinois. He is the former co-founder and co-principal of a STEM-focused magnet academy, also in Illinois, where he developed curricular programming that included engineering courses, dual-credit high school classes in English language arts (ELA) and mathematics, computer coding, and foreign languages. He has been an educator since 2008, with experience as a teacher, co-principal, and principal, gaining all his experience in low-income school districts that primarily serve students from minority backgrounds. He has also instructed graduate-level courses on best practices in the ELA classroom and on designing and implementing literature circles in junior high ELA.

Dr. Entsminger is an active member of several professional organizations, including the Illinois Principals Association, Illinois Association of School Administrators, and ASCD. In 2024, he was honored with the Administrator Award for Meritorious Service by the Illinois State Board of Education.

His leadership and learning philosophy are grounded in the belief that relationships are the foundational pillars for all learning. He advocates for using the responsive circle process to help students manage and resolve conflicts, which he believes cultivates a culture of prevention. Dr. Entsminger also establishes cultures of high expectations that have helped his schools make impressive gains in student achievement. He has presented throughout the United States on topics ranging from responsive circles and conflict management to integrated project-based learning.

Dr. Entsminger holds a bachelor's degree in mass communication from Illinois State University, a bachelor's degree in English secondary education from Governors State University, a master's degree in school leadership from Concordia University Chicago, and a doctorate in curriculum and inquiry from Northern Illinois University.

To book JR Entsminger for professional development, contact pd@SolutionTree.com.

Introduction

If a child doesn't know how to read, we teach. If a child doesn't know how to swim, we teach. If a child doesn't know how to multiply, we teach. If a child doesn't know how to drive, we teach. If a child doesn't know how to behave [or resolve conflict], we punish.
—Tom Herner

With the advent and popularity of social media, the average person gets a glimpse into public and private school classrooms around the world on a daily basis. Shorts, reels, posts, and videos show schools like never before. At times, we see exhilarating learning led by engaging classroom teachers. Other times, we see school leaders cultivating positive school culture by facilitating exciting assemblies or activities. To be sure, there are some amazing things happening in our schools every day. On the other hand, we've also seen some disturbing videos showing excessive conflict in schools, including student-on-student, student-on-adult, adult-on-student, and adult-on-adult conflict.

Obviously, some important context may be missing from these videos and news stories. More often than not, these videos or news stories purposefully exclude important contextual information. Nevertheless, these reports and images are upsetting, and unfortunately, these upsetting scenarios and situations can make the goal of educating and learning more challenging, which often leads to increased stress and burnout for educators. It can be a vicious cycle.

Most educators have a plethora of theories as to why student misbehavior and conflict are prevalent in schools, such as the following.

- Lack of parental involvement or poor parenting
- Increased use of social media and technology
- COVID-19 pandemic and resulting remote learning
- Poverty
- Violent media
- Idolization of poor public role models
- Increased societal polarization

More than likely, it's probably a combination of these issues. For instance, research indicates a negative impact of social media and technology on the brain, on mental health, and on decision making (Buda, Lukoševičiūtė, Šalčiūnaitė, & Šmigelskas, 2021; Liu & Ma, 2020; Valdez, Thij, Bathina, Rutter, & Bollen, 2020; Zhang et al., 2023; Zhao & Zhou, 2020). What's more, researchers have found a connection between early childhood experiences with poverty and later conduct disorder (Holz et al., 2015). In 2022, 11.6 million children lived in poverty in the United States (The Annie E. Casey Foundation, 2024). Clearly, educators don't have control over many of the aforementioned theories, as most of those issues happen outside of school. However, there is something educators can control.

Former president of the National Association of State Directors of Special Education Tom Herner is attributed with saying, "When students can't read, we teach them. When students can't write, we teach them. When students can't add or subtract, we teach them. But, when students can't behave [or, in this case, manage and resolve their conflicts], we punish them." Combined with all the external issues perpetuating conflict, the traditional ways we help students process, manage, and resolve their conflicts tend to make matters worse. Most times, rather than teaching and helping students through conflict, educators punish students for engaging in conflict-inducing behavior.

The punishments students receive usually have the following negative impacts.

- **Excludes them from the school community:** Many believe removing students who misbehave from the educational environment would improve the environment and quality of education for other students. However, exclusionary discipline has a demonstrated negative impact on overall school culture and climate, even for the students who are not in detention, suspended, or expelled (Nese et al., 2020).
- **Puts them on a path toward future problems:** Students who experience exclusionary school discipline practices, such as suspensions and expulsions, often have problems later in life, including increased misconduct, future academic difficulties, and run-ins with the law (Marchbanks et al., 2014; Novak, 2018; Wolf & Kupchik, 2017).
- **Fails to address the underlying issues:** Many schools use exclusionary discipline in an effort to make schools safer and deter repeated behavior. However, exclusionary discipline does nothing to make schools safer, often exacerbates misbehavior, and may even retraumatize students because it does not pay attention to the underlying issues, such as trauma and generational poverty (Dutil, 2020; Fisher & Hennessy, 2016; LiCalsi, Osher, & Bailey, 2021).

There is hope. There is hope because students do care. We just have to help them show it. There's hope because there aren't many families, if any, that don't want what's best for their children. We just have to help them show it. There is hope because the education field is full of professionals who care deeply about the well-being of students.

There's hope because there is a better, more effective way to help our students process and resolve conflict. This method includes students *and* adults. It helps students learn, grow, and prepare for more productive futures. It teaches them a variety of important life skills they'll use now and in their future. It helps them better understand their past and present. It helps them properly process and address the conflict in their everyday lives.

This method—responsive circles—is the best way forward. Briefly, *responsive circles* provide a structured, systematic means of resolving conflict, leading to better behavior and decision making among students, a more positive school culture and climate, and the cultivation of a culture of prevention (Costello, Wachtel, & Wachtel, 2019; Diliberti & Schwartz, 2023; EAB, 2023; Mills, Barocas, Butters, & Ariel, 2019; Strang, Sherman, Mayo-Wilson, Woods, & Ariel, 2013; Wang, 2023). The core purpose of this book is to equip K–12 educators with practical strategies and tools for implementing and using responsive circles, which fosters positive relationships among students, staff, and the community and promotes restorative practices. By resolving student conflict in a way that teaches empathy, ensures accountability, and builds community, educators can transform student behavior and create a supportive, inclusive school culture.

Responsive Circles: History and Efficacy

Responsive circles, rooted in Indigenous traditions and restorative justice, have a notable past that honors the collective healing and community building practices of diverse cultures, such as the First Nations in Canada and the Navajo Nation (Brown, 2001; Perez & Romkema, 2022). These practices emphasize the importance of productive conflict resolution and relationship building (or mending) through involvement, accountability, and empathy. This book is written in reverence to the originators of these restorative traditions, aiming to carry forward their wisdom while adapting and making practical the principles for modern K–12 school settings. By building on these foundational practices, educators today can create inclusive spaces that prioritize connection, understanding, and growth.

History

Like restorative practices, the history of circles is traceable to Indigenous peoples. Circles or similar community-based conflict resolution practices have been used by a variety of Indigenous tribes around the world. Indigenous communities in Canada, collectively known as First Nations, have a long history of using circles to address conflicts and promote healing (Borrows, 2010; Ross, 2006). These communities are instrumental in influencing the development of modern restorative justice approaches in Canada.

In the United States, the Navajo Nation has long used traditional peacemaking practices known as "Hozhooju Naat'aanii" or "the Beauty Way" to address disputes and restore balance and harmony within the community (Bluehouse & Zion, 1996). In Australia, various Aboriginal communities have used circle-based processes as part of their justice and conflict resolution practices. The Indigenous Sami people in Scandinavia have a tradition of using community circles to address issues and conflicts within their communities, emphasizing dialogue, understanding, and collective decision making. For many Indigenous peoples, these practices often reflect the deep cultural values of collective responsibility, community involvement, and restoration that have been passed down through generations: "We're all in need of help. And helping others helps us at the same time" (Pranis, 2005, p. 6).

In the context of modern restorative practices, circles are a "powerful process to proactively build bonds and community," and they "provide a forum to respond to conflict and wrongdoing" (Costello et al., 2019, p. 22). What's more, "the underlying philosophy of circles acknowledges that we are all in need of help, and that *helping others helps us* at the same time" (Pranis, 2005, p. 6). As a symbol of connection, fairness, support, and inclusion, circles are naturally inviting places, and they are effective for facilitating open and respectful communication regarding conflict and disagreement. Because circles offer an opportunity to address conflict head-on, they help participants repair relationships and address the root causes of conflicts. What's more, circles are naturally efficient. Many societies and groups have used circles as a means of efficiently and effectively sharing a message among a group of individuals.

Efficacy

For the purposes of this book, the following language and definitions are used. As you work—with staff, families, students, and community members—it will be important to make clear what words and phrases mean. This can help avoid unnecessary politicization and inaccurate connotations that diminish the focus.

- ○ ***Restorative justice*** seeks to address conflict with a focus on repairing harm caused by wrongdoing rather than simply punishing the wrongdoer. This approach, which involves all parties affected by an offense, attempts to identify and address harms, needs, and obligations in order to promote healing (Zehr, 2015). This approach invites all members of the community, including both victims and offenders, to engage in a dialogue and collaboratively find solutions. (Read more about word choice on page 82.) Overall, restorative justice is the broader concept or guiding philosophy that underpins both restorative practices and restorative discipline.

- ○ ***Restorative discipline***, a specific application of restorative practices in the context of schools or educational settings, seeks to address student misbehavior by fostering belonging instead of exclusion and accountability over punishment (Evans & Vaandering, 2016). Instead of relying solely on punitive measures like suspensions or expulsions, restorative discipline seeks to address behavioral issues by fostering understanding and repairing relationships. This approach helps students learn from their mistakes, take responsibility for their actions, and reintegrate into the school community. The word *discipline* may connote a myopic focus on misbehavior and punishment, whereas restorative *justice* and restorative *practices* first focus on relationships and then provide an alternative to discipline and traditional punishment.

- **Restorative practices** are the set of tools, strategies, and techniques that embrace the restorative justice philosophy and can be applied in various settings. These settings often include schools, workplaces, and the broader community. The practices help build and strengthen relationships, create a positive community culture, address conflicts and wrongdoing in a proactive and inclusive manner, and cultivate empathy. Essentially, being restorative means ensuring those most directly involved in a conflict are the people to resolve it (Costello et al., 2019). Restorative discipline is regularly applied in schools, workplaces, and communities to build positive relationships and social capital. Restorative practices' heavy focus on relationships and community building is more proactive than reactive. This helps make restorative practices more preventive as well as responsive.

Overall, you can remember that although they are similar in belief and approach, *restorative justice* focuses on addressing harm after wrongdoing, *restorative discipline* applies restorative justice principles specifically to school discipline, and *restorative practices* are both proactive and responsive, aiming to foster community and relationships before and after harm occurs.

Efficacy research on responsive circles suggests the following benefits.

- **Reduces traditional punitive disciplinary measures:** Circles offer an alternative to traditional punitive approaches, promoting more constructive and rehabilitation-focused responses to conflict. Traditional punitive disciplinary measures that exclude students from school put students and the entire school community at risk of low school achievement and increased dropouts (Augustine et al., 2018).
- **Contributes positively to relationship building:** In well-structured circles that have clear expectations, students develop respect and appreciation for their differences and how each person individually contributes to the power of the group. In schools where strong, positive teacher-student, student-student, and teacher-teacher relationships exist, students exhibit higher academic achievement and are often more motivated and engaged in class. What's more, these relationships positively contribute to the overall school and classroom atmosphere (Wang, 2023).
- **Helps cultivate and maintain positive school and workplace climate:** Circles help develop positive and supportive climates and cultures in both schools and workplaces. With widespread teacher shortage and retention issues, coupled with the rise in student behavior problems, cultivating positive school and workplace climates is important (Diliberti & Schwartz, 2023; EAB, 2023).

- **Reduces power structures:** Traditional settings where seats are arranged in rows naturally direct attention and authority to the one at the front. At certain times and during certain situations, this may be necessary. However, there's limited power in a circle, if any at all. This may help participants feel more comfortable and empowered when it comes to sharing their experiences or their knowledge and often makes students more likely to make positive change because those in authority do restorative work *with* students, rather than *to* students. What's more, responsive circles shift the focus away from exclusionary disciplinary measures that typically reinforce traditional power dynamics. Finally, in the circles themselves, power imbalances are dismantled when all voices are heard and valued (Costello et al., 2019; Klevan, 2021; Smith, Fisher, & Frey, 2015; Wang & Lee, 2019).
- **Enhances soft skills development:** As active members in the problem-solving process, participants practice active listening, affective communication, and conflict resolution, which can improve their overall communication skills. Participants also develop self-regulation and empathy, which improve creative abilities and critical thinking skills. In addition, when students feel empathy from their teachers, this enhances the sense of belonging in a school and classroom setting, thereby further positively impacting the school culture and climate (Cai, Yang, Ge, & Weng, 2023; University of Cambridge, 2021).
- **Increases shared accountability:** With exclusionary discipline, students are simply removed from the school environment without having addressed other participants or repairing the harm they caused. However, in well-structured circles with clear expectations, all participants have a chance to play a role in the circle outcome. Participants are encouraged to take responsibility for their actions, collaboratively address conflicts, and work to repair any harm done. Involving all participants in a conflict—those who caused harm and those affected by harm—encourages collective responsibility and accountability (Costello et al., 2019).

In addition to relationship building and positive culture development, consistently using responsive circles helps cultivate prevention: prevention of repeated conflict-inducing behaviors, prevention of rehashed relational breakdowns, prevention of social-emotional dilemmas, and prevention of school dropouts and subsequent issues. Three distinct aspects of the responsive circle process cultivate prevention (and are missing from traditional punishment): (1) a chance to learn how to safely and productively resolve conflict, (2) relationship nurturing and repair, and (3) empathic modeling and questioning throughout.

If used correctly, responsive circles have the power to transform school environments. Responsive circles empower students and staff to address issues collaboratively, repair harm, and build stronger, more connected school communities. The practical guidance offered in this book can help educators effectively enact long-lasting cultural change.

Book Audience and Organization

This book is crafted specifically for educators, with a focus on those who are directly involved in resolving student conflict, improving student well-being, and shaping school culture—K–12 teachers, social workers, guidance counselors, and school leaders. It acknowledges the unique challenges these professionals face and offers practical strategies for implementing and facilitating responsive circles and building more inclusive and supportive learning environments. These educators will find valuable insights into how they can use responsive circles to address conflict and emotional and behavioral challenges, foster resilience, and develop social-emotional skills such as empathy. What's more, school leaders are offered practical suggestions and guidance for integrating these practices into the broader school context, ensuring restorative approaches become a core part of the school's ethos.

I tried to ensure this book gives you something practical to use in your classroom, in your office, or in your school the following day. Each chapter starts with an anecdote based on professional experience. The names and identifying characteristics of anyone real are changed. The inclusion of these anecdotes serves multiple purposes: to humanize complex concepts or ideas, to offer an engaging chapter commencement, to demonstrate areas for practical application, and to inspire or motivate you, the reader.

The upcoming chapters are delineated here. Reading this book from start to finish in chronological order is highly recommended. But, if you want to get rolling with the responsive circle process as soon as possible, here's the suggested order: chapter 3, chapter 4, chapter 1, chapter 2, and chapter 5.

- **Chapter 1, "Important Things to Remember About Student Behavior":** This chapter provides a foundational understanding of student behavior, emphasizing that behavior is a form of communication and that adult perceptions and biases, trauma, and the influence of technology and social media all play significant roles in shaping student actions and reactions in the school environment.

- **Chapter 2, "Traditional Punishments Versus Consequences":** This chapter explores the key differences between traditional punitive measures and meaningful consequences, highlighting how common disciplinary practices like detentions, suspensions, and expulsions mostly fail to address the root causes of behavior and often exacerbate issues.

- **Chapter 3, "Responsive Circle Facilitation":** This chapter provides a detailed guide for facilitating responsive circles, outlining the critical steps that occur before, during, and after the circle process to ensure productive conflict resolution.

- **Chapter 4, "Circle Types and Tools":** This chapter introduces the various circle types and structures, along with the specific tools that aid facilitation and the language that guides meaningful dialogue and ensures all participants feel heard and respected during the process.

- **Chapter 5, "Resistance and Resource Constraints":** This chapter addresses the common challenges schools face when implementing responsive circles, focusing on overcoming resistance, managing resource limitations, and empowering leaders and change agents to drive successful, sustainable adoption of restorative practices.

This book also has repeating discussion questions and next steps at the end of each chapter. These questions help encourage reflection, promote understanding regarding the application of concepts, and seek to engage you. What's more, these questions can help if you're leading a team through collaborative learning on responsive circles, including but not limited to a book study or book club. Similarly, I included information on next steps to promote more understanding regarding practical application, check and assess current reality and progress, facilitate planning, and support continuous learning and growth. Both the discussion questions and next steps help make the content in this book more actionable and results oriented, ensuring you leave each chapter with a better understanding and planning ideas for growth and improvement.

CHAPTER 1

Important Things to Remember About Student Behavior

After lunch, before heading back to their classrooms, students stopped at their lockers to grab books and supplies for afternoon instruction. Because I was helping with lunch duty, I helped a few stragglers get where they needed to be. I saw a student, accompanied by a teacher, slam his locker shut in obvious agitation. As I walked toward the two, I saw the student hit Mr. Garcia on the arm. The student didn't hit Mr. Garcia very hard. And the teacher quickly moved on as if nothing happened. When we made eye contact, Mr. Garcia waved me away, as if to say, "Don't worry. I got this."

Later in the day, I asked Mr. Garcia about the incident. He assured me everything was fine; he had taken the student's iPad, which served as the student's communication tool. The student had limited verbal skills. Mr. Garcia explained to me that, by hitting his teacher, the student was communicating that he could no longer communicate because his device was taken away. "No consequences were necessary," said Mr. Garcia. "The behavior was my fault."

I learned an extremely valuable lesson that day. I learned that we communicate our needs in different ways and that when someone can't communicate their needs for whatever reason, they work to have their needs met in other ways. I learned student behavior is multifaceted and there are many simultaneously interacting variables that impact a person's behavior on any given day. For instance, a student may display problematic behavior due to a variety of issues, including illness, attention deprivation, family disputes, and adjustment or developmental dilemmas. Reflecting on our own behavior as educators is important for understanding how others respond. I learned that knowing our students, like the way Mr. Garcia knew this particular student, is essential. I also learned that moving on from these types of experiences, though not always easy, is important for everyone involved. That way, we minimize letting them shape our interactions with students.

This anecdote highlights a critical lesson about communication, particularly when working with students who have limited verbal skills. The situation illustrates that behavior serves as a form of communication, especially when traditional means of communication are unavailable. Mr. Garcia recognized that the student's behavior—hitting his arm—was not an act of aggression but an expression of frustration after losing access to his communication device. By reflecting on his own actions and understanding the root cause of the student's behavior, Mr. Garcia avoided unnecessary consequences, focusing instead on the student's underlying needs. The experience emphasizes that educators must be attuned to the diverse ways students express themselves, particularly when they face barriers to communication. It also underscores the importance of knowing students individually, as this insight enables educators to respond with empathy and understanding. Moreover, moving on from such incidents without holding on to them is crucial for fostering positive future interactions. This story illustrates the importance of reflection, flexibility, and maintaining a compassionate, student-centered approach in education. This chapter covers the following topics.

- Behavior as communication
- Adults misperceiving behavior and having biases about it
- Trauma's impact on behavior
- Technology and social media's impact on human development

Behavior Is Communication

When I collaborate with groups of educators on behavior and classroom management, I always start by collecting some experiential information. I ask participants to share an experience they've recently had with student behavior. This brief discussion activity always elicits typical but passionate responses. Most times, educators laugh and talk about a recent humorous encounter with a student. I often share that during my first year as a principal in a new district, a fifth-grade student wrote "Dr. E is Cool" with a permanent marker on a bathroom stall. When a teacher brought it to my attention, I immediately found it comical, and it was definitely good for my ego. But, it was still an instance of damaging school property. Other times, educators cry and recount deeply traumatic events that have changed them in some way. During one session, a teacher shared how she was bitten by a primary student in her classroom and how it impacted her life at home with her own children. Either comical or serious, the activity is enlightening, and most educators share experiences centered on behaviors like name-calling, theft, bullying, fighting or other physical aggression, destruction of school property, instances of disrespect toward adults, and dishonesty.

At this point, I ask educators to notice I said nothing of "misbehavior." I simply asked them to recount and share experiences with student "behavior." Participants usually look around the room, smile, and shake their heads in agreement. All our responses gravitated toward misbehavior. We all *chose* to focus on instances of student misbehavior.

When I ask adults to share an experience of student behavior, I've honestly never had anyone share something positive or routine. No participant has ever shared how their student successfully engaged their behavior intervention plan or how a student efficiently put away their things in their hallway locker and safely returned to their seat in the classroom. No participant has ever shared how one of their students effectively and efficiently took their scheduled calming corner break and then quietly returned to their seat. No participant has ever shared how their student met their self-awareness goal for the day and received a positive phone call home from the principal. When we hear "student behavior," we often automatically assume it's "misbehavior," and that generates many memories and emotions.

Behavior is normal, whether it is good or bad behavior, and we demonstrate different behaviors all day long, many times without even knowing it. For example, whether it is in workshops, faculty meetings, or at fun school events, how we sit and where we sit communicates something. During an after-school faculty meeting where I planned to discuss a recent uptick in conflict-inducing behaviors at recess, I purposefully sat with a group of teachers in the middle of the room. I exaggerated the way I was sitting in order to attract attention. I wanted staff members to see me. I yawned. I coughed out loud. I put my interlocked hands behind my head and leaned back in my chair. By the looks on their faces, I could tell my staff thought it was pretty strange. After a minute or two, I stood up and walked toward the front of the room. I stood at the front of the room and asked if they noticed anything about my behavior. Many said I seemed impatient and uninterested.

"Bingo," I said. I commented on how they noticed my posture and some of my nonverbal gestures and how these things wordlessly communicated my feelings. I gave an example of how the position of our legs and feet actually give insight into our personalities. I pointed out how sitting with knees straight may communicate confidence and honesty while sitting with crossed legs may communicate a defensiveness or a closed-off mindset (Sharma, 2023). I explained that seating arrangements or choices communicated comfort and safety. We often congregate or sit in areas or near individuals where we feel safe and comfortable. I explained that when I yawned, I could have been communicating sleepiness or boredom—or, as some researchers theorize, I yawned to wake myself up or make myself more alert (Medical University of South Carolina, n.d.). I reminded my staff that many times throughout the day, we engage in powerful forms of nonverbal communication. In fact, much of the forms of nonverbal communication we engage in often send underlying messages we know nothing about or even understand. Finally, I asked staff to reflect on whether there was something our students were trying to tell us based on their recent conflict-inducing behavior at recess. This primed us all for good dialogue focused on the fact we had just returned to in-person learning after the COVID-19 pandemic and that many students needed to be reminded about how to properly and safely play at recess.

The *theory of behavioral communication* suggests that individuals may express their feelings, needs, and thoughts through behavior rather than more direct, open, and verbal communication. Some people, whether consciously or unconsciously, tend to engage in more behavioral communication despite having the ability to engage in verbal communication (Ivanov, n.d.; Ivanov & Werner, 2010; Morin, 2023).

There are four types of communication behaviors (UK Violence Intervention and Prevention Center, n.d.).

1. **Aggressive:** People demonstrating aggressive communication behavior tend to engage in personal attacks and put-downs, and they may use intimidation to get their needs met. Aggressive communicators may feel inadequate and lack empathy. Aggressive communicators who have trouble with verbal communication may exhibit nonverbal behaviors such as ignoring, standing over, or rushing other people.

2. **Assertive:** People demonstrating assertive communication behavior often have the ability to express their desires and feelings appropriately. Assertive communication can also be expressed through nonverbal behaviors. Assertive people convey openness and receptivity in their body language with an upright posture and relaxed movements. Assertive communicators make appropriate eye contact, and when they do engage in verbal communication, they do so with a clear tone of voice.

3. **Passive:** Passive communicators often internalize their feelings in order to avoid conflict and discomfort. People engaging in passive communication may internalize their feelings because they feel their needs don't matter, and if they speak up, they'll be rejected. Passive communicators who struggle with verbal communication may exhibit nonverbal behaviors such as actively avoiding confrontation, sighing a lot, fidgeting, avoiding eye contact, exhibiting a hesitancy to speak, and making themselves small in stature.

4. **Passive-aggressive:** People demonstrating passive-aggressive communication behavior express their negative feelings or frustrations indirectly, often through subtle or ambiguous actions. In everyday life, they may feel powerless, stuck, or resentful. Passive-aggressive communicators avoid direct eye contact, use exaggerated body language like rolling their eyes, may be purposefully unreliable, tend to sulk during conversations, and can have a deflated posture.

While a person might show more than one of these four behavioral communication styles, it's rare for someone to use all four of them.

Again, behavior is a form of communication, and we all communicate our needs in different ways. Even as adults, we may communicate our needs or wants in an unexpected manner. For our students, especially the ones who don't know any better or the ones who have difficulty with verbal communication, the way they communicate their needs may seem a little unconventional. When students can't verbally communicate what they want or need, they may engage in aggressive communication behaviors that are extremely unexpected or uncalled for in a given situation.

Adults May Misperceive and Have Biases Regarding Student Behavior

Perceptions have the potential to shape the way we approach and interact with our students. Whether consciously or unconsciously, we all develop perceptions regarding our students, especially when it comes to academic ability or behavior. For instance, when a student experiences difficulty with a certain topic or skill, we formulate perceptions based on this difficulty. Let's say a student struggles with addition. We may develop perceptions about this particular student regarding their overall mathematical ability, their future mathematical progress, how they will perform on certain assessments, and what types of supports they may need. On one hand, you could call these *reactive perceptions*—reacting to external stimuli in the environment. On the other hand, perceptions can also be proactive. If no observable stimuli are present, we may generate proactive perceptions based only on the stimuli we have observed prior.

As educators, if we let perceptions shape our expectations for our students, how we develop relationships and connections with our students, how we educate our students, or how we create learning environments that support our students, this can negatively impact student outcomes (Gilakjani & Sabouri, 2017; Gupta & Sampat, 2021; Harste & Burke, 1977; Hattie, 2023). Similar to implicit bias, though perceptions can be unintentional, they still affect our judgments, decisions, and behaviors. Even more alarming, perceptions regarding student ability or behavior can cause health consequences for educators—increased stress, anxiety, worry, exhaustion, and burnout (Kokkinos, Panayiotou, & Davazoglou, 2005; Tsouloupas, Carson, Matthews, Grawitch, & Barber, 2010; Wettstein et al., 2023).

One seventh-grade science teacher expressed anxiety regarding the upcoming school year. She mentioned that while reading her class lists a few days prior, she noticed the names of three students whose reputations preceded them. She described how she heard about the students fairly often in the staff lounge. We briefly conversed about misperceptions and how it was important to give them a chance. I also reminded her that she's a different educator than the teachers who had worked with these students in the past.

However they occur, we often hold perceptions about students before they even arrive in our classrooms. Most of the time, the perceptions we hold about students, especially about students who have never even been in our classrooms, should be referred to as *misperceptions*. These types of misperceptions shape the way we interact with students, often negatively impacting potential future relationships and connections. Responsive circles help school community members productively resolve conflict and build and maintain relationships. However, if we don't check our own perceptions (or misperceptions) first, the potential for responsive circles to help build relations may be limited.

Trauma Impacts Behaviors

Trauma is an emotional and psychological response to a distressing or deeply disturbing event or experience, such as an accident or a natural disaster (American Psychological

Association, n.d.). For some, it may be caused by a single event, like an act of violence. For others, it may be caused by repeated exposure to traumatic events. Experiencing a traumatic event has the potential to overwhelm a person's ability to cope (Rice & Groves, 2005). Complex trauma exposure "refers to the simultaneous or sequential occurrences of child maltreatment—including emotional abuse and neglect, sexual abuse, physical abuse, and witnessing domestic violence—that are chronic and begin in early childhood" (Blaustein et al., 2003, p. 5).

Adverse childhood experiences (ACEs), which are traumatic or stressful events that occur during childhood and have a significant impact on a person's physical and mental health throughout life, can be an example of complex trauma exposure (Sprenger, 2020). The pandemic, specifically the many underlying issues resulting from the pandemic (social isolation, disrupted routines, the deaths of family members, sudden job loss and economic hardship, parental stress and mental health, and health-related anxiety), is an example of widespread ACEs. Educators and families report that students are noticeably different since returning from a year of remote learning: anxiety issues, behavior issues, organizational and executive function issues, and academic issues are more common (Williams, 2023). You name it, many of our students are now in the throes of it (not to mention the impact on all of the adults around them). This is the result of collective trauma and increased personal trauma directly related to COVID-19—deaths, evictions, and increased food insecurity, for example.

In the mid-1990s, Vincent J. Felitti and Robert F. Anda, in partnership with the Department of Preventive Medicine at Kaiser Permanente and the Centers for Disease Control and Prevention, conducted research to investigate a potential link between children's emotional experiences and their subsequent mental and physical health (Felitti et al., 1998). According to their findings, ACEs were much more prevalent than previously thought, and they discovered that adverse childhood experiences do indeed correlate with adult health. At the time of the study, Felitti and his colleagues (1998) identified the following categories as ACEs.

- **Physical abuse:** Physical harm or injury inflicted by a parent or caregiver
- **Emotional abuse:** Repeated patterns of negative verbal or emotional interactions, such as humiliation or belittlement
- **Sexual abuse:** Any form of unwanted sexual contact or exploitation experienced during childhood
- **Neglect:** Failure to provide a child with basic needs such as food, shelter, clothing, or emotional support
- **Household dysfunction:** Exposure to various types of dysfunction within the household, including domestic violence, substance abuse, mental illness, or parental separation or divorce

In the 2010s, researchers have found that ACEs are just as prevalent, if not more common, around the world (da Silva & da Costa Maia, 2013; Kalmakis, Shafer, Chandler, Aponte, & Roberts, 2018; Kreatsoulas, Fleegler, Kubzansky, McGorrian, & Subramanian,

2019; Malvaso, Delfabbro, & Day, 2019). In fact, one study suggests that almost half of all children from the United States from newborn through seventeen have experienced at least one ACE (Crouch, Radcliff, Brown, & Hung, 2019).

Reactions to trauma often vary but can include unpredictable emotional responses, difficulty concentrating, prefrontal cortex impairment, neurotransmitter imbalances, memory issues, fatigue, depression, avoidance, flashbacks, and suicidality (Bielas et al., 2016; Bremner, Vermetten, Afzal, & Vythilingam, 2004; Guest House, 2019; Maniglio, 2011; MIT Health, n.d.; Samuelson, 2011; van der Kolk, 1989; Walker, 2014; Widom, DuMont, & Czaja, 2007). Trauma impacts the body immensely. The original ACEs study found that participants exposed to childhood emotional abuse, physical abuse, sexual abuse, and household dysfunction were at an increased risk of developing severe obesity, ischemic heart disease, chronic lung disease, skeletal fractures, liver disease, and cancer (Felitti et al., 1998). Children, for instance, are at immense risk of developing cardiovascular disease, obesity, diabetes, migraines, and chronic obstructive pulmonary disease after experiencing severe instances of early life stress, as well as increased risk of developing dangerous habits like alcohol and drug abuse and smoking (Nemeroff, 2016).

Mitigating these deleterious effects requires an integrated approach, and there are a variety of strategies that, when implemented in a systematic way, help ameliorate some of the lifelong consequences resulting from ACE exposure (Jimenez, Wade, Lin, Morrow, & Reichman, 2016; Sprenger, 2020). Building, maintaining, and nurturing relationships with caring adults can be instrumental in alleviating the impact of ACEs. These relationships can provide emotional support, guidance, and a sense of stability (McDonald, Kingston, Bayrampour, & Mail, 2015). Creating opportunities for students to engage with their social networks, including friends, extended family members, or community organizations, allows more sources of emotional help and health. Helping students foster and nurture these connections provides students with a variety of support channels and avenues (Merrick et al., 2019).

Providing students with mental health guidance from therapists, counselors, social workers, and psychologists can also assist in processing and addressing the emotional and psychological effects of ACEs. This type of support can help students develop or rebuild coping mechanisms that promote peace and healing. Additionally, it helps to raise awareness about ACEs. Many schools and districts benefit from training on the early identification of ACEs, prevention, and trauma-sensitive or trauma-informed practices (Gomis-Pomares & Villanueva, 2020; Jacob et al., 2019; Merrick et al., 2019; Thakur et al., 2020). Schools can also work with local, regional, or national agencies to ensure their students and families have access to essential resources like healthcare, nutrition, safe housing, and robust educational opportunities. And, in the classroom, students benefit immensely from resilience-building activities like mindfulness exercises, physical activity, creative outlets and projects, and participation in extracurricular activities (Jacob et al., 2019).

In well-designed and effective responsive circles, students with trauma can build trust, safely express their emotions, engage in healing, strengthen their relationships with others, and develop self-regulation and other coping skills.

Technology and Social Media Impact Human Development

As an exhausted parent, I can't tell you how many times I've thought about simply handing my toddler an iPad while at a restaurant so I can enjoy some semblance of a normal night out. Just a few minutes of screen time. Maybe it will help keep her occupied just so I can eat. To my dismay (but probably to our toddler's benefit), my wife, who's also an educator, never allows it. Never a big fan of screen time, she believes children "must learn to be bored." She believes children should make use of their potent imaginations while they're young. In the long run, I'm sure she's right. I'm sure it would be helpful for our child to learn to be bored. I'm sure it'll be beneficial for our child to make use of her robust imagination. But just a little screen time can't be that bad, right?

The impact of technology and social media on the brain, which can subsequently influence behavior, is attracting more and more attention, especially regarding how it affects children. Clearly, there are benefits associated with technology use (Torkington, 2024; UNICEF, 2024). Despite the upsides, researchers found the following impacts of digital technologies and social media on the brain.

- **Digital addiction:** Excessive use of technology, particularly smartphones, can lead to addictive behaviors, impacting attention spans and overall well-being (Salicetia, 2015).
- **Reduced attention and focus:** Constant exposure to digital devices can contribute to decreased attention spans and difficulties in maintaining focus on tasks (Oaten, 2024).
- **Sleep disruptions:** The use of screens before bedtime can disrupt sleep patterns, leading to sleep deprivation and negative impacts on cognitive function (LeBourgeois et al., 2017).
- **Physical health issues:** Excessive use of technology can lead to sedentary behavior, which can negatively affect physical health and contribute to various health problems (Bull et al., 2020).
- **Impaired social skills:** Excessive reliance on digital communication may lead to reduced face-to-face social interactions, potentially impacting social skills and emotional intelligence (Alonso & Romero, 2017).
- **Brain structure changes:** Some studies suggest that excessive screen time can lead to structural changes in the brain, particularly in regions associated with attention and memory (Takeuchi et al., 2016, 2018).
- **Increased risk of self-inflicted violence:** In an exceptional situation of social isolation such as the global pandemic, children and adolescents may be more vulnerable to self-inflicted violence when using the internet intensively (Deslandes & Coutinho, 2020).
- **Mental health concerns:** Heavy use of social media and exposure to negative online content can contribute to feelings of anxiety, depression, and loneliness (Shakya & Christakis, 2017).

- **Increased anxiety and stress:** Excessive use of social media can contribute to anxiety and stress due to the fear of missing out (FOMO), cyberbullying, or comparing oneself to others (Blasco, Cosculluela, & Robres, 2020; Hunt, Marx, Lipson, & Young, 2018; Kinser et al., 2021).
- **Addiction:** The constant engagement with social media platforms can lead to addiction or addiction-like behaviors (Andreassen, 2015; Blasco et al., 2020).
- **Self-esteem and self-perception issues:** Spending too much time on social media can negatively influence a user's self-esteem (Kalpidou, Costin, & Morris, 2011).
- **Decreased real-life interaction:** Spending too much time on social media may reduce face-to-face interactions, leading to potential social isolation and feelings of loneliness (Song et al., 2014).

Technology and social media use have impacted our students' development, which has consequences for their behavior in our schools and classrooms. In thoughtfully structured responsive circles, students who've experienced decreased real-life interaction because of technology have a space to reconnect with adults and peers in the school community. Students with reduced attention and focus or technology addiction may develop important self-regulation skills. Students with impaired social skills because of technology overuse can rebuild social skills like active listening, empathy, and collaboration.

Either with your team or on your own, respond to the discussion questions and consider what next steps to take with the following guidance.

DISCUSSION QUESTIONS

Imagine you're in a collaborative team meeting, and many of the members of the team are hypothesizing why a group of students engaged in a certain behavior. How would you help navigate this conversation?

Can you think of a time when you developed (mis)perceptions about students? Did these misperceptions cause you to treat them differently? What are some ways educators can prevent themselves from developing misperceptions about their students?

Can you share an example from your experience when you or a member of your team recognized trauma was immensely impacting a student's academic or behavioral development? How did you and your team help resolve this situation?

Reflecting on the challenges faced by students and educators post-pandemic, what are some important considerations for understanding and addressing student misbehavior during this time?

In your current setting, how are students allowed to use technology in school? Should the policy be more restrictive regarding technology use? Why or why not?

NEXT STEPS

Build a guiding coalition. If you haven't done so already, organize a guiding coalition of staff members to help with a variety of activities, including drafting a new vision and mission that highlight restorative practices and responsive circles for building school community and resolving conflict.

Facilitate open dialogue. During a staff meeting, allow educators to share their experiences regarding student behavior and perceptions. This platform is for honest dialogue about how misperceptions form and how they can be addressed.

Reflect and journal. During a staff meeting, encourage personal reflection through journaling. Educators can reflect on their own potential biases, perceptions, and experiences with students and track how they may adjust their responses in the future.

Learn more about trauma-informed practices. Work with the guiding coalition and other staff to learn more about trauma-informed practices and how they can be implemented into classroom and school culture.

Review technology policies. Collaboratively revisit your school's technology policies to evaluate whether they strike a balance between learning and overuse. If necessary, consider proposing policy changes that prioritize both digital literacy and student well-being.

Do ongoing observation and adjustment. Regularly observe students' behavior, relationship building, and conflict resolution. Use restorative practices and responsive circles to continuously refine how the school community addresses behavior and promotes a healthy, balanced learning environment.

CHAPTER 2

Traditional Punishments Versus Consequences

I got a radio call asking me to report to a teacher's room because she needed help. Mrs. Petty was waiting for me in the hallway. She was distraught.

"He won't do anything. Even after I talked to his parents, he still won't do anything. Classwork. Homework. Nothing. I tried talking with him. I tried praising him for work completion. I tried rewarding him for having his homework done. I tried calling his parents when he did nothing. I tried withholding Fun Friday from him. I tried everything in my classroom. I need you to step in."

This wasn't the first time a teacher asked me to intervene when a student wasn't completing assignments. I was fully prepared to have a nice conversation with the student in hopes of first identifying what was causing the behavior and then motivating him to do his work. My positive relationship with the student made me feel even more confident about my ability to reach him with a conversation.

The teacher confirmed that my intention was only to converse with the student and expressed her dissatisfaction with that.

"He needs a consequence. He needs to know that this kind of behavior is not acceptable. He needs to know that while he's in my class, the expectation is that he completes his work," she explained.

I followed up by asking what kind of consequence she had in mind. She suggested perhaps not allowing recess for a day or asking him to serve a detention.

I realized I could help in an additional way. I needed to explain the purpose of and reality behind many traditional disciplinary measures and behavior strategies, including disallowed recess and detention, as well as explain the difference between consequences and punishments.

If educators ask themselves what the purpose of any disciplinary measure or behavior strategy is, it is likely to align with teaching students a lesson. In a simplified way, teaching a lesson and creating a safe school environment are certainly desirable outcomes for disciplinary measures.

When students engage in conflict-inducing behavior, we want them to learn a lesson. In fact, we want them to learn that lesson so well they never engage in that particular conflict-inducing behavior again. Also, depending on the situation, I'm sure many educators, especially administrators, have employed a disciplinary measure to create or ensure a safer environment at school. But, in reality, the purpose of any disciplinary measure or behavior strategy is even more straightforward than "teaching students a lesson." We employ disciplinary measures and behavior strategies to change behavior.

Now, focus on the different behavior measures or strategies you use in your current setting. Perhaps something like this comes to mind: "Per the directive from my superior (maybe a director of special education or special services), I follow what's in the IEP (individualized education program) or BIP (behavior intervention plan)," or "I've resorted to suspensions for serious offenses." Some educators use a variety of methods in their classrooms, like managing through proximity, point or incentive systems, and phone calls home. Some leaders involve their school resource officers in certain situations, especially physical altercations. Some alternative school administrators, who are often trained by organizations that specialize in managing disruptive or aggressive behavior, employ verbal de-escalation strategies before resorting to physical intervention.

Now think carefully and, without judging yourself or the current system, assess if the kinds of disciplinary measures you use truly teach students a lesson. Do these strategies or systems teach students something beyond a reward or consequence, or teach students to behave better when faced with similar circumstances in the future? Do students learn to make better decisions because of disciplinary consequences? Employing or modeling de-escalation techniques may help in the moment, but do students learn something from them, and can they replicate the techniques on their own later or when not prompted by an adult? Then, consider the questions in table 2.1. If the answer is yes, you'll see the indicators in the right column in your school.

We all want students to learn a lesson after they make a poor behavioral decision. But, if we're being honest, the discipline strategies used in many schools and classrooms today don't involve students, hold students accountable for their actions, allow all participants to be heard, or ensure resolution. Put plainly, they don't teach students a lesson. In fact, a lot of the time, those discipline strategies are most correctly defined as *punishments*—something that is imposed or inflicted on others to induce pain or suffering.

Responsive circles serve as a form of *consequence* rather than punishment because they focus on repairing harm, ensuring accountability, and building understanding rather than imposing or inflicting pain and suffering. Actually, I go as far as saying that responsive circles are the natural consequence, the mature consequence, or the real world consequence of a poor behavioral decision. When mature adults make mistakes, we gather to talk it out.

Table 2.1: Judging Your System's Efficacy

QUESTIONS TO CONSIDER	INDICATORS IN THE AFFIRMATIVE
Do these measures make your school safer?	Reduced classroom consequences, office referrals, and exclusionary disciplinary measures like suspensions; improved staff survey results regarding school culture, climate, and safety
Do the measures involve students (or the person who initiated the conflict) in the process?	Students involved in formal and informal conflict resolution processes
Do students take accountability for their actions?	Students taking responsibility, verbally or via actions, after receiving some kind of consequence or punishment
Is there closure (a sense of emotional and psychological resolution) for staff and students involving understanding, acceptance, and feeling valued after an incident when you employ current strategies?	Results from student surveys regarding consequences or punishments used in the classroom or schoolwide reveal psychological safety (trust, willingness to be vulnerable) from a majority of participants
Is the conflict resolved in a healthy, productive way?	Reduced repeated conflict-inducing behavior; reduced classroom or schoolwide consequences or punishments

Whether it's a mistake among family, a mistake among friends, or a mistake in the workplace, we gather to talk about it. When adults make a mistake, they talk through the mistake and learn from it. Now, consider the difference between punishment and consequence.

Distinguishing Between Punishment and Consequences

Some educators use the terms *punishment* and *consequence* interchangeably. But, there are some pretty significant differences between the two that we'll explore in this section. Where punishments are passive, consequences are *considerate*, and they put *responsibility* on the person who engaged in conflict-inducing behavior (Costello et al., 2019).

Defining Punishment

Like most things in education, people define punishment very differently. Some educators feel strongly about how they define punishment, how they view punishment, and how they use punishment. But, in this book, we define and understand *punishment* as follows: the authorized and intentional imposition of something unwanted on an individual. This imposition usually consists of something that causes undesirable pain, suffering, hardship, or burden. A punishment is typically imposed on an individual, most often the offender, after the offender has violated some type of rule, law, expectation, or norm. Because punishment causes harm, it would seem reasonable to assume that an individual would try to avoid it (Hanna, 2008; McPherson, 1967; Scribner & Warnick, 2021).

A defining feature of punishment is its expressive function. The *expressive function* holds that punishment sends a very public message of disapproval of a behavior to the offender and the entire community (Scribner & Warnick, 2021). Punishments shame and humiliate offenders, and it's the public shame and humiliation that communicate disapproval. Some feel that traditional school punishments that "send a message" are necessary because many school-approved behavior measures lack an expressive function (or that the expressive function of school-approved behavior measures is not strong enough to properly communicate disapproval; Duff, 2001). For instance, as part of a progressive discipline system, the first offense may result in a verbal warning. Some feel that a verbal warning is not strong enough to communicate disapproval. The expressive function associated with a verbal warning won't match the seriousness of the misbehavior in the eyes of the student, the school, and the community. The punishment must fit the crime, so to speak. Or, more precisely, the public message sent by the punishment must be equally powerful as the message sent by the crime.

In addition, punishments are *passive* (Costello et al., 2019). They are imposed on others with the intention of inflicting pain or suffering (Hanna, 2008; McPherson, 1967; Nelsen, 1996). In the school context, let's not think of pain and suffering in the most literal and physical sense (although, it should be noted, corporal punishment is still legal in nineteen U.S. states, and of those nineteen states, three of them still regularly use it; Scribner & Warnick, 2021). In the school context, pain and suffering may involve some extremely tedious or frustrating task. As an example, many schools make students write something over and over again during after-school detention. The thought is that boring a student with a menial task will discourage future misbehavior.

When it comes to punishment's expressive function, it's important to remember that we work with children. Children are still learning. They're still growing. Their brains are still developing. They don't have the problem-solving capabilities or conflict resolution abilities adults have (or should have). Take the situation with Mrs. Petty at the start of this chapter. I ended up having a serious conversation with the student, just like I planned. For many students, having a serious yet private conversation like this is strong enough to send the message that a behavior is unacceptable. The serious yet private conversation lessens or eliminates shame and humiliation, keeps a student's dignity intact, and provides a chance to learn more about the child's life and experiences.

Because shaming or humiliating students hurts relationships, it's also bad for school culture and climate (Perry, 2019). Shame and humiliation are extremely toxic and infectious. When unchecked, this approach can quickly spread through an entire department or grade level (Smith et al., 2015). Furthermore, because punishment is passive, it often only works "superficially, primarily when the misbehaving students are in view of those in authority. . . punishment does not create empathy in students or encourage them to internalize a commitment to behave properly" (Costello et al., 2019, p. 62). Why would students develop empathy or internalize a commitment to behave better when they're not involved in the resolution process?

Because there are no opportunities to develop life skills like empathy and there is no commitment to internalization, punishments rarely reduce recidivism or "reoffending" and rarely create safer school environments (Costenbader & Markson, 1998; Hemphill, Toumbourou, Herrenkohl, McMorris, & Catalano, 2006; Leung-Gagné, McCombs, Scott, & Losen, 2022; LiCalsi et al., 2021; Mittleman, 2018; Morgan, Salomon, Plotkin, & Cohen, 2014; Novak & Krohn, 2021; Schreck, Miller, & Gibson, 2003; Skiba, 2013; Weingarten, 2015; Wiley, Slocum, O'Neill, & Esbensen, 2020; Winter, 2016).

None of this is to say that students don't deserve some type of corrective action, especially after they've engaged in egregious conflict-inducing behavior. However, it's important to remember that corrective action need not always take the form of punishment, especially if said punishment shames and humiliates students or if it neglects to teach anything. After all, "Not every form of punishment deters every form of behavior" (Scribner & Warnick, 2021, p. 23).

Before administering corrective action, it's helpful to ponder Campbell F. Scribner and Bryan R. Warnick's (2021) reflective questions on punishments from their book *Spare the Rod: Punishment and the Moral Community of Schools.*

1. Is there evidence that specific threats of punishment deter specific problematic behaviors among students? For example, is there reliable evidence to suggest that the specific punishment of suspension will prevent the specific problematic behavior of fighting?
2. What evidence exists to suggest that punishment is truly *the only way* to deter these behaviors? For instance, is suspension truly *the only way* to deter fighting? Or are there other, less exclusionary measures that work?
3. If this punishment truly deters these behaviors, are there any unintended consequences that stem from their use, such as negative impact on the school-student relationship or school-community relationship?
4. How likely is it that the punishment will change the behavior in the long term?

It's also important to draw a distinction between punishing children and punishing adults. Many of us might agree that if punishments were reserved only for those adults who knowingly and freely chose to do something wrong, that would be one thing. Ideally, we would punish adults who we assume have the average ability to consider alternative courses of action, weigh the pros and cons of their decision making, and comprehend the repercussions of their choices but still decide to do something wrong. When applying this logic and our definition of punishment (the imposition of harm or hardship on another) to children, it sounds a little different. The "imposition of harm or hardship" on children sounds a little unethical. Maybe even immoral.

Consider a phrase such as, "They should know better." Then consider the multitude of variables in a person's development that may or may not make that the case.

- **Do students have the ability to consider alternative courses of action?** Research suggests that though early elementary-age students can begin to weigh alternatives in decision making, their ability to do so improves significantly as they grow. Studies suggest that children start to develop the cognitive frameworks for considering alternative courses of action around early adolescence (Jin, Ji, & Peng, 2019; Morelli, Casagrande, & Forte, 2022).
- **Do they have the ability to simultaneously weigh the pros and cons of their decisions?** Research suggests that younger children, especially those under the age of twelve, tend to struggle with evaluating outcomes and simultaneously weighing complex alternatives (Jin et al., 2019; Morelli et al., 2022).
- **Do they have the ability to look beyond the decision and truly comprehend the repercussions that follow?** Research suggests that brain maturation, particularly in areas responsible for decision making, occurs gradually, with full maturation typically not being achieved until a person's mid-twenties. For example, even teenagers who may be capable of some rational decision making struggle to consistently consider the long-term consequences of their actions because of the underdevelopment of their prefrontal cortexes (Abrams, 2022; Haidt, 2024).
- **If, after weighing pros and cons and comprehending the repercussions, are they able to identify an alternative action?** Because of the underdevelopment of the prefrontal cortex, which is essential for executive function, future planning, and impulse control, younger children often rely on simple strategies. What's more, children mostly respond and adapt to feedback from their environments rather than proactively identifying and considering potential outcomes (Jin et al., 2019; Morelli et al., 2022).

With that in mind, do students really "know better"? Based on the research, it is safe to say they are developmentally incapable or limited in their abilities around decision making. However, even if educators are aware of the research and studies regarding brain development, in tense situations involving student conflict, it may be hard to remember this information because the focus is often on resolving the situation. Nevertheless, a person cannot behave better unless they are *taught* better. Students won't behave better unless they're taught better. Even when students struggle with trauma, disabilities, illnesses, or language barriers, educators can teach students a better way through responsive circles; they can learn how to resolve conflicts, manage and maintain relationships, empathize, move on from disagreements and fights, and avoid future conflict.

After taking a closer look at punishments, it's time to dive into consequences and how they differ from punishments.

Defining Consequences

Responsibility is one of the keys to consequences. Passive punishments are imposed without requiring action or reparation on the part of those who engaged in the conflict-inducing behavior. "One of the most persistent myths in school discipline is that punishment is a way of 'holding students accountable.' However, punishment relies on external control and only works when the authority is watching" (Costello et al., 2019, p. 77). It's not the passive punishment that holds students accountable. A true consequence requires action on the part of those who engaged in conflict-inducing behavior. It's a considerate consequence that involves students in the resolution process and holds them accountable.

As an example, a sixth-grade student hits another sixth-grade student at recess and receives a detention as punishment for it. After he serves the detention, educators hope the behavior stops. The two students are never brought together for resolution. Now consider a consequence: students *are* brought together for conflict resolution. They are encouraged to process their behavior and their emotions. The facilitator assists them in repairing any harm done. The students make collective commitments for improving their behavior, making better decisions, and preventing the same issue from happening again. They are educated about different decisions they could make instead and get support making them in the future. There's reparation. There's forgiveness. There's closure. Most importantly, there's learning. I discuss the reparation and resolution process more in chapter 4 (page 71).

Some educators contend that natural consequences or natural effects in school-based situations where students engage in conflict-inducing behavior are inauthentic. They argue that educators can't truly or effectively simulate a natural consequence for students in our school settings. This perspective misses the point. The point shouldn't be to make the consequences as natural or authentic as possible (though it couldn't hurt). The point is to help students learn something after engaging in conflict-inducing behavior, take responsibility for their actions, resolve their conflicts with others in a way that maintains dignity and relationships, and ultimately cultivate prevention.

Revealing How Punishments Miss the Point

Punishments in schools have long been employed as a means to manage student behavior and maintain order. As mentioned, these school punishments often include detentions, suspensions, and expulsions, and they are aimed at addressing infractions like classroom disruptions, tardiness, insubordination, violence, and more. Let's review the history and effectiveness of detentions, suspensions, and expulsions.

Current Practices and Their Historical Backgrounds

School punishment has a long history. In early American schools, educators claimed the purpose of punishment was to cultivate the development of responsible and independent citizens. To cultivate responsible and independent citizens, punishment sought to develop in students a sense of efficiency, organization, and morality. At the time, educators often used religion to justify punishment as a means of developing morality. In fact, many early educators saw punishment as a way to bring children into accordance with divine authority (Scribner & Warnick, 2021). Nevertheless, since its inception, punishment in schools has always been wrought with fiery debate. From corporal punishment to more progressive and social-emotional-focused approaches, differing sides have fought and argued over which measures are truly best for students and school communities. We will focus on three very popular punishments, also referred to as "traditional disciplinary measures": detentions, suspensions, and expulsions.

Detentions

Detention in schools goes back a long way. Although its exact origins are difficult to pinpoint, early documentation shows it was used in the late 1800s in the Danish elementary school system (de Coninck-Smith, 1997). Initially, it was referred to as the *detention cell* or the *little confinement* and served as the temporary placement or confinement of students who'd been neglected by their parents. In addition to housing neglected children, detention was also used to reduce truancy and absenteeism. At the time, truancy was considered the "worst crime a child could commit against the school" (de Coninck-Smith, 1997, p. 79). The purpose of detention was to punish students through the application of strict discipline and deprivation of freedom. Danish educators believed that the punishment in detention would bring about "salvation" for the truant pupil and that isolation would change the pupil's behavior. Interestingly, educators at the time were also concerned with prevention, and they believed confinement in detention would prevent "wicked examples" from proliferating. As a byproduct of the confinement, it was hoped detention would save all the other students from the "moral contagion" carried by the "truant pupils" (de Coninck-Smith, 1997, p. 82). While confined in detention cells or detention homes, often for days or weeks at a time, the students (nearly all boys) worked. Their work depended on the season. In the summer, they toiled away outside in the gardens during the day and cleaned and cooked inside at night. During the winter, they produced cottage industry articles while laboring away in attic workrooms. Educators at the time believed these students would learn a strong work ethic in detention and that their employment was protection against trouble.

In terms of the effectiveness of detention in late 1800s Denmark, a halt in "incipient degeneracy" was only "sometimes" achieved; when it came to prevention, Danish school records suggest "something over half [of the boys in detention] had later brushes with the authorities" (de Coninck-Smith, 1997, p. 82). Like many traditional disciplinary measures used in current schools, detention then disproportionately impacted certain groups of students. Danish documents suggest there were as many truant girls as there were truant boys. However, boys were most often confined in detention, and 99.9 percent of the boys in detention also came from the lowest socioeconomic status stratum in Copenhagen society (de Coninck-Smith, 1997). Despite its popularity and longevity, very little current reliable research exists regarding the effectiveness of detention. We do know that detention is common in the public education system of the 21st century. Detention remains the most popular and widely used response to disciplinary infractions, as American elementary and secondary public schools issue tens of millions of detentions every year (Dignity in Schools Campaign, n.d.; Spaulding et al., 2010).

Because schools and educational leaders have differing philosophies on punishments and consequences, the duration and what students do during detentions can vary widely. Though what they do during detention may differ, students are typically expected to complete assignments, read in silence, write as a punishment, or sit with their heads on their desks. For *certain* students, some evidence suggests that detention can help decrease future behavior issues. Those students are usually the ones who are *unlikely* to repeatedly break school rules in the first place (Infantino & Little, 2005). When it comes to considering what works for the majority of students, detention is not an effective discipline tool. Detention is especially ineffective for those students often referred to as "frequent fliers," or students who repeatedly receive infractions. In those cases, detention might actually *increase* the recurrence of student misbehavior or even function as a reward (Atkins et al., 2002).

Out-of-School and In-School Suspensions

Similar to detentions, suspensions, whether in school or out of school, are intended to reduce student misbehavior. Out-of-school suspension (OSS) involves completely removing a student from school grounds and school-sanctioned activities, including but not limited to sporting events and dances.

In-school suspension (ISS) is a disciplinary measure where students are temporarily removed from the classroom for a behavior issue and are supervised by a staff member on school grounds (Smith et al., 2021). Unlike OSS, the purpose of ISS is to keep students in the learning environment and process, usually by having a staff member supervise the suspended student while they complete assignments for the duration of the ISS. Occasionally, students serving ISS may have time to discuss their behavior with deans, counselors, or social workers. From 1973 to 2010, national suspension rates climbed quickly, reaching their highest point ever in 2010; since then, suspension rates have declined as a result of the Obama administration working to reduce the amount of exclusionary discipline used in public schools (Gregory, Osher, Bear, Jagers, & Sprague, 2021; Leung-Gagné et al., 2022). Some national estimates indicate that OSS rates decreased by approximately 20 percent between 2011 and 2013 (Office for Civil Rights, 2016). Though the number of suspensions in American public schools is declining, it still remains high. For example, during the 2015–2016 school year, K–12 schools issued 2.7 million out-of-school suspensions to students (Office for Civil Rights, 2018). As another example, during the COVID-19 pandemic in the 2020–2021 school year, around 2.5 million students—approximately 5 percent of the total student population—experienced out-of-school suspensions (Burr, Kemp, & Wang, 2024).

Originally, suspensions were used to address more serious disciplinary infractions and inappropriate behaviors. This often included physical aggression and drug, alcohol, or tobacco use on school grounds. In a hierarchical discipline system, suspensions usually come after detentions. However, with the Gun-Free Schools Act of 1994, which mandated expelling students who brought firearms to school, zero-tolerance measures, especially suspensions, began being used more frequently to address a variety of seemingly minor offenses, including verbal disrespect and profanity toward staff (Costenbader & Markson, 1994; Dupper, 1998; Leung-Gagné et al., 2022).

The effectiveness of school suspensions as a disciplinary measure has always been a topic of ongoing debate. While suspensions may temporarily remove disruptive or potentially harmful students from the school environment, research suggests they're not an effective long-term solution for addressing behavioral issues or improving student outcomes. Educators regularly express concern with suspensions because they (1) remove students from the general education environment, (2) may actually increase instances of poor or antisocial behavior, and (3) never actually address the underlying issues that cause student misbehavior in the first place (Ambrose & Gibson, 1995; Costenbader & Markson, 1998; Hochman & Worner, 1987; Noltemeyer, Ward, & McLoughlin, 2015; Sautner, 2001; Weingarten, 2015; Winter, 2016).

In regard to lost instructional time, the U.S. Department of Education (USDOE) issued a report regarding federal discipline data that found, in a single academic year, there was a loss of 11 million instructional days due to out-of-school suspensions (LiCalsi et al., 2021). The USDOE concluded that the learning loss resulting from these out-of-school suspensions is most prevalent among secondary students. Students in high school lose instruction at rates five times higher than students in elementary school (LiCalsi et al., 2021). Equally alarming, in-school suspensions, which many educators believe to be less detrimental than out-of-school suspensions, perniciously impact student academic performance and learning. This is not surprising, as ISS removes students from the classroom, resulting in the loss of valuable instructional time and hands-on support from the teacher.

Research suggests that receiving just one in-school suspension puts students at greater risk of academic failure on state standardized tests (Smith et al., 2021). Graduation rate, another student outcome, is also impacted by suspension. Researchers have found that the probability of being on track to graduate drops for students who are removed from the instructional environment due to suspension (Balfanz, Byrnes, & Fox, 2015; Noltemeyer et al., 2015; Rumberger & Losen, 2016). What's more, because they exclude students from the learning environment, research suggests suspensions leave students feeling alienated and unsupported, and they become even more disconnected, disengaged, and antisocial (Arcia, 2006; Fabelo et al., 2011). When students feel disconnected and disengaged from their school community, the likelihood of problematic and antisocial behaviors increases.

Research also demonstrates that preexisting behavioral problems are exacerbated when students are suspended (Quin, 2019). This means that for the students who exhibit problematic behaviors, suspending them from school removes them from school protective factors like trustworthy adults and increases exposure to outside risk factors like more antisocial peers.

Moreover, educators are right to be concerned that suspensions don't address the underlying issues of student misbehavior. Simply removing students from the environment for misbehavior does nothing to address the reasons for the misbehavior. This approach creates zero opportunities for students to learn the appropriate behaviors or how to safely and productively resolve conflicts (Leung-Gagné et al., 2022; LiCalsi et al., 2021). Suspensions may immediately remove a student from a problematic or dangerous situation, but they do nothing to help students process their trauma, develop coping or regulation strategies, or cultivate conflict resolution skills. If the underlying issues for behavior problems aren't addressed, it's unlikely that behavior will change (Hannigan & Hannigan, 2024). Prevention can only be cultivated if the true issues for behavior problems are addressed. Prevention cultivation only works if students are included as part of the resolution process.

Expulsions

Schools often use expulsion as a tool for maintaining a safe and productive learning environment, as it removes students who may pose a threat to others or who repeatedly engage in disruptive or harmful behavior. Like most behavior measures, the use of expulsion depends on a variety of contextual variables, including the school setting, the people in charge of handling disciplinary matters, the circumstances, and the individuals involved. From 1974 up through 2006, expulsion rates in American schools more than doubled. Approximately 28,300 students in K–12 public schools were expelled during the 2020–2021 school year (U.S. Department of Education, 2023).

However, similar to other exclusionary discipline measures like suspensions, expulsions disproportionately impact racial minorities, students in special education, and students from low socioeconomic backgrounds (LiCalsi et al., 2021; Liu, 2023; Owens & McLanahan, 2020; Raffaele Mendez & Knoff, 2003; Skiba et al., 2011). Research often finds that students of color are more likely than White students to be expelled for any offense; what's more, boys of all races and students with disabilities are disproportionately expelled from school compared to their peers (U.S. Department of Education, 2023). Results also suggest students of different ethnicities and students of color are more likely to receive more serious consequences than their White peers for the same infraction (Skiba et al., 2011). It should be noted that, though expulsion rates are declining, there are state- and district-level variations, with some districts showing much higher rates depending on local policies and enforcement of zero-tolerance practices (U.S. Department of Education, 2023).

In addition to rampant disproportionality, expulsions never address the underlying issues for student misbehavior. What's more, expulsions place students at increased risk for negative outcomes, including lower achievement levels, an elevated risk of school dropout, involvement in delinquent activities, contact with the juvenile justice system or incarceration, increased distrust in adults, and decreased academic and employment opportunities (Brown, 2007; Ekstrom, Goertz, Pollack, & Rock, 1986; Finn & Servoss, 2014; Raffaele Mendez & Knoff, 2003; Skiba, 2013; Skiba & Rausch, 2006; Wald & Losen, 2003). Most educators posit that, like suspension, expulsion should be used as a last resort, with a focus on rehabilitation and addressing the root causes of problematic behavior. Similar to students who receive suspensions, students who are expelled lose out on valuable instructional time, causing them to fall behind academically and socially. And, like with all zero-tolerance policies, most researchers and policymakers advocate for other, less exclusionary types of disciplinary measures.

Unintended Consequences of Traditional Discipline

In addition to research-based shortcomings regarding their effectiveness, there are also unintended byproducts resulting from the use of traditional disciplinary measures. As mentioned, one of the most obvious and major detractions of traditional disciplinary measures like detentions, suspensions, and expulsions is the lack of learning opportunities. Not only do these measures remove students from the school community, but they also remove students from any conflict resolution process. As a result, students involved in the conflict don't get the chance to come together and work toward resolution and closure. No learning happens when these measures are used.

Traditional disciplinary measures also harm relationships (Tuff, 2023). School environments and the social interactions in them have the power to build trust, cultivate connections, and develop shared experiences for teachers and students (Kirk, 2009; National Center on Safe Supportive Learning Environments, n.d.). It's important to understand how educators manage relationships and how conflict impacts schools and those within them. All day, every day. What's more, some research suggests that students who experience severe traditional disciplinary measures may internalize deviant or delinquent labels and identities, which can cause subsequent poor and antisocial behavior. Students who develop these types of identities or labels tend to disassociate themselves from prosocial students, withdraw or isolate themselves, and increase their contact with other students who've internalized the delinquent labels and identities (Lemert, 1951; Wolf & Kupchik, 2017).

The use of traditional disciplinary measures also leaves a wake of rampant inequity.
- o According to the National Center for Education Statistics, during the 2013–2014 school year, Black students (13.7 percent) were suspended at rates double or triple that of their peers (de Brey et al., 2019).
- o Black and Indigenous students were expelled from school at a rate of 0.4 percent, while all other groups, including Hispanic, Pacific Islander,

White, and Asian students, were expelled from school at a rate of 0.2 percent combined (de Brey et al., 2019).

- Like race-based discipline disparities, a similar disparity exists for students with disabilities (Achilles, McLaughlin, & Croninger, 2007; Brobbey, 2018; Fabelo et al., 2011; Zhang, Katsiyannis, & Herbst, 2004). The number of out-of-school suspensions for students with disabilities more than doubles that of students without disabilities (Office for Civil Rights, 2016).
- Students with disabilities were punished using suspensions or expulsions at more than twice the rate of other students, even when they were involved in the same types of infractions as their non-disabled peers (Lacoe & Manley, 2019).
- Exclusionary disciplinary methods disproportionately impact students from different economic backgrounds, too. Research shows that students from low socioeconomic status backgrounds are suspended or expelled at higher rates than their more advantaged peers (Achilles et al., 2007; Fabelo et al., 2011; Morgan et al., 2019; Rumberger & Losen, 2016).
- The utilization of traditional disciplinary measures and the resulting disproportionality also result in the dramatic loss of instructional time for Black students (Losen & Martinez, 2020). Black students lose almost five times the amount of instruction as White students (Álvarez, 2020; LiCalsi et al., 2021).
- Some researchers posit that the discipline gap, which is the phrase used to describe the suspension and expulsion disparities between races, is a major factor contributing to the achievement gap and the racial or gender-based academic inequality prevalent in U.S. public schools (Álvarez, 2020; Gregory, Skiba, & Noguera, 2010; LiCalsi et al., 2021; Losen & Martinez, 2020; Morris & Perry, 2016; Osher, Cantor, Berg, Steyer, & Rose, 2020; Smith et al., 2021).
- These disparities are present in other countries as well. In 2023, data from Australia showed that Indigenous students, who comprise only 11 percent of the student population, accounted for 26 percent of all school exclusions (Down et al., 2024).
- Similar trends can be seen in Canada, as well. In provinces like Ontario, suspension rates are higher for Indigenous students, Black students, and students from low socioeconomic backgrounds (Ahmed, 2024; Ma, Mumphrey, & Lurye, 2024).

Unfortunately, even when controlling for typical factors that increase dropout rates, studies show that suspensions and expulsions, especially of students from low socioeconomic backgrounds, often lead to school dropout and disengagement (Balfanz et al., 2015; Noltemeyer et al., 2015). As a result, the use of these traditional disciplinary measures has also resulted in the perpetuation of the school-to-prison pipeline. The pipeline encapsulates various policies, processes, and practices that are allegedly responsible for the increased likelihood of student involvement in the criminal justice system after experiencing punitive disciplinary measures in schools. For instance, *suspension* is the single most important predictor of school dropout—more important than poverty—and of a path toward unemployment, reliance on social welfare, and incarceration, which feeds the school-to-prison pipeline (Flannery, 2015). The pipeline represents a failure to address students' underlying needs, provide equitable educational opportunities, and support the holistic development of our students.

Responsive circles offer a powerful alternative to exclusionary discipline.

Either with your team or on your own, respond to the discussion questions and consider what next steps to take with the following guidance.

DISCUSSION QUESTIONS

What do you believe is the purpose of any disciplinary measure or behavior strategy? Whether you're in the classroom or the building administrator's office, do the disciplinary measures or behavior strategies you use satisfy that purpose? How do you know?

How involved are students in your classroom or school? In what ways are they involved in the learning process? The conflict resolution process? Are there opportunities to increase their involvement? Explain.

Imagine you're having a conversation with a colleague about how a third-grade student misbehaved in front of the whole school at a recent assembly. She advocates for the child to receive more severe "consequences" than those administered. How would you navigate this conversation?

Have you personally witnessed any of the unintended byproducts of traditional disciplinary measures (lack of learning opportunities, minimal student voice and choice opportunities, increased antisocial behavior or other conflict-inducing behavior, negative impacts on school culture)? If so, have you done anything to ameliorate those byproducts? Explain.

NEXT STEPS

Begin creating a more restorative culture. Host open discussions and reflective sessions to explore the impact of exclusionary discipline on students, especially marginalized groups. Then, analyze the benefits associated with restorative practices and responsive circles. Finally, begin developing a shared restorative vision with the school community, including members of the guiding coalition, other educators in the building, administrators, parents, and students. The vision should emphasize the importance of inclusivity, relationship building, and accountability.

Start small by piloting. It would be unrealistic to go fully restorative or start using responsive circles for every discipline or conflict in your school. Trained professionals don't even use responsive circles to address every conflict. Instead, pick a single grade level or a few students who regularly engage in conflict-inducing behavior and start considering more restorative alternatives to the exclusionary discipline they normally face. It could be responsive circles, guided reflections, or another restorative conflict resolution strategy. Whatever you do, it helps to just get started.

Engage families. Keep the families in your community informed. Educate parents about restorative practices and responsive circles so they understand how these practices benefit their children. Encourage parents to support the processes at home. You could even hold family informational sessions to explain the restorative vision you're creating and the eventual goal of moving toward a more restorative culture.

CHAPTER 3

Responsive Circle Facilitation

"Yo, Dr. E," a voice called to me in the hallway. I turned to see a student named Mark with whom I had a positive rapport; he had participated in a few responsive circles before, and when I saw him, we sang a song that related to his name. This time, Mark didn't sing. He didn't laugh. He didn't give me the typical high five. I assured him I was there to help and that we could figure things out.

Instead, he quietly but very quickly explained what he was upset about. "At lunch, we were talking about what we're wearing on spirit day, and Yusuf made a comment about my jersey, so I made fun of his new haircut. He got super angry and called me a few names. When we were at recess, he came up to me, got in my face, swore at me, and then pushed me. I pushed him back. I know I shouldn't have. But I did. Then, Mrs. Gomez broke it up."

I explained that I was sorry to hear about the incident and praised him for letting me know what happened.

He interjected before I could say anything else. "I was hoping that we could do one of those circle things—me, you, and Yusuf. Yusuf is my friend. But I think we hurt each other's feelings, and I need your help to fix it."

I gave Mark a hug and said, "Dude, I'm so proud of you. Absolutely, buddy. We'll circle up ASAP."

This was a momentous occasion. I could barely contain my excitement. This student was concerned about upsetting or disappointing a trusted adult, and he cared about repairing a friendship because he understood the damage that had been done. What's more, he was up front about his part in the ordeal. Years prior, getting any responses from him, let alone hard truths and taking responsibility for his involvement in negative situations, was nigh impossible. In the past, he had been reluctant to participate and would initially lie about his involvement in student conflict. Finally, and probably most importantly, Mark sought out help to address the conflict before it escalated into something more serious. He used skills and processes we'd been working on for years to resolve a conflict. Circling was working!

This encounter marked a turning point in Mark's growth—not just in terms of his ability to manage conflict, but in his willingness to seek help and take responsibility for his actions. Someone who was once reluctant to engage in conflict resolution had become a young person who understood the importance of repairing relationships, and he actively sought out the tools to do so. Mark's proactive request for a responsive circle not only demonstrated his maturity, but it also validated the power of the process. Years of effort in cultivating these skills had paid off, and this was a moment where the potential of restorative practices truly shone.

As we move into this chapter, we take a closer look at responsive circles—the tool that helped Mark navigate his conflict. We explore how these circles foster communication, accountability, and healing and why they are so effective in transforming conflicts into opportunities for growth and understanding. I explain the important steps that circle facilitators must consider before actually facilitating a circle (especially their first circle). I elaborate on the specific stages of the responsive circle process, providing you with a guide for facilitating responsive circles on your own. This is just the beginning of understanding how circling can reshape not only individual relationships and decision making, but also the broader school culture.

Remember, there's no cure for conflict. There never will be, and there shouldn't be. People disagree. They have conflicting goals. They have misunderstandings that can be resolved, and even when they cannot be, open communication can still lead to resolution rather than escalation. Sometimes, conflict can be productive and serve as a profound learning opportunity. Responsive circles help facilitate that. You help facilitate that. Addressing conflicts head-on in a healthy way creates an environment where students feel heard instead of ignored and supported instead of alone. This reduces the likelihood of repeated conflict and misbehavior (Darling-Hammond, 2023; Wang & Lee, 2019).

Prior to the Responsive Circle

Before facilitating a responsive circle, conduct some prep work. The better the preparation, the smoother the circle. When the focus is on resolving a conflict, things in general can be a little bumpy, which makes a smooth circle even more important. To prepare for a responsive circle, educators (whether they are administrators, social workers, or classroom teachers) must consider context; investigate; meet individually with each student; keep families informed; schedule the meeting; identify the right setting; determine the circle structure; decide whether to use a talking piece and which one to use; develop or choose norms; and decide roles.

Consider Context

Circles work well with students of all ages. However, there are some important things to remember about circles in certain contexts. For example, students in early elementary grades (K–2) probably need a little more support, especially with things like vocabulary, norms, and expectations. Spending too much time explaining vocabulary such as *analyze* and *prevent* may take the focus away from the purpose: repairing harm, resolving conflict, and reintegrating. Or, you might use the steps exactly as they appear regardless of the participants' ages. You could see this as an opportunity to teach academic vocabulary. This also works, as long as the process, not the parlance, is the focus.

Vocabulary adaptations may include the following.

- **Harm:** Hurt
- **Analyze the harm:** Research
- **Repair the harm:** Fix it
- **Prevent future harm:** It won't happen again
- **Collective commitments:** Promises
- **Reintegration:** Welcome back

Developing norms for early elementary students is important, too. When doing so, be direct and concise. Some examples of norms for early elementary students follow.

- Take turns speaking.
- Use kind words.
- Be honest.
- You can pass.

These norms help set expectations for behavior and participation, fostering an environment where young students can share and listen in a structured, respectful way. Remember, it's important to revisit these norms regularly and reinforce them with visual reminders or prompts during circle time.

Investigate

Facilitators always conduct an investigation before convening a circle. They speak with students involved in order to get a better understanding of what happened. While investigating, facilitators should take very detailed notes. These notes help paint a picture of what happened, when it happened, why it happened, how it happened, and to whom it all happened.

Meet Individually

After conducting the initial investigation, the facilitator meets individually with each student who was harmed. During this meeting, the facilitator briefly discusses the harm the student experienced, the plan to facilitate a responsive circle, and how the facilitator's goal is to help all parties resolve the conflict. The facilitator asks if students are interested in participating and clarifies that the circle is a safe place where all input is valued and respected. To not make those who experienced harm uncomfortable, the facilitator reminds them that their participation is voluntary.

If they choose to participate and the plan is to move forward with the circle, the facilitator reminds students that, if at any time they feel unsafe or uncomfortable, they must speak up, and the facilitator can pause or end the circle. When discussing participation with a student who has experienced harm, the facilitator can use one of the scripts in figures 3.1, 3.2, or 3.3 (pages 40 and 41). The first script is for elementary students.

> Good morning, friends! Today, we have a special opportunity to come together and share in something called a responsive circle. Now, many students in our school have participated in circles before. Some have not. So, let me tell you why it's such a wonderful thing to be a part of.
>
> With responsive circles, we all sit together in a big, safe space. We use this time to talk about how we feel, any problems we might be having, or even things that make us really happy. And the best part is—you share *only* if you want to. You don't have to talk if you don't feel ready, and that's totally OK. What's important is that we are all here to listen to and support each other.
>
> We're going to use something special called a talking piece. When it's your turn to hold it, you can share what's on your mind. And while someone else is speaking, we all practice listening with our whole bodies—that means our eyes, our ears, and our hearts are focused on the person speaking.
>
> In our circle, we follow some very simple rules. We speak kindly to each other, listen carefully, and treat each other with respect.
>
> These circles help us work through any problems or tough feelings. They make our school a happier, safer place where we understand and take care of each other.
>
> Remember, joining the circle is your choice. No one will be upset if you decide to just listen today. We're all here to support each other, and every voice matters. I hope you'll join us!

Figure 3.1: *Elementary-level responsive circle participation script.*
Visit **go.SolutionTree.com/behavior** *for a free reproducible version of this figure.*

As students get older, they can take on more responsibilities in circles. For example, depending on the experience of the middle school participants, one student might share the script in figure 3.2 with their fellow classmates before participating.

> Hey, everyone, thanks for coming together today. I wanted to talk to you about something really important—something that can help us all work through challenges, support one another, and build a stronger sense of community. It's called a responsive circle.
>
> I know that middle school can be tough. Maybe you've had a disagreement with a friend or someone is not treating you nicely. Responsive circles are a space where you can share those thoughts in a safe, respectful environment. And the best part? You're not alone. We're here to listen.
>
> Here's how it works: We'll sit in a circle—no one is above or below anyone else—and we use a talking piece to take turns. When you have the talking piece, it's your turn to speak. And when someone else has it, it's your turn to listen. You don't have to talk if you don't want to. This is a voluntary space, and your voice will always be respected here.

> The circle is about more than just talking—it's about connection. We're not here to judge anyone or point fingers. We're here to understand each other, to resolve conflicts, and to offer support.
>
> So, if you're interested in participating today, I encourage you to give it a try. Remember, joining is totally up to you—but I think it's a really positive experience. And I'll be here to guide the process.

Figure 3.2: *Middle school–level responsive circle participation script.*
*Visit **go.SolutionTree.com/behavior** for a free reproducible version of this figure.*

At the high school level, I encourage a participant to read the script in figure 3.3 with their fellow classmates before participating.

> Good afternoon, everyone. I want to talk about something valuable that we're offering here at school—responsive circles. High school is a stressful time. You're dealing with homework, friends, family, and life in general. We all go through things that can weigh us down. Sometimes, those stresses can lead to conflict or misunderstandings, and that's where responsive circles come in.
>
> In our responsive circle, we come together to talk openly about what's going on in a respectful and supportive environment. It's a safe place where you can share what's on your mind, where you can listen to others, and where we work through challenges without judgment. The circle is about healing and moving forward. If there's been a disagreement, a misunderstanding, or if something just feels off between you and someone else, this is a chance to talk it out in a way that's constructive, not confrontational.
>
> Being in high school means you're on the path to adulthood, and part of that journey is learning how to communicate effectively and solve problems in a mature way. In the circle, everyone gets a turn to speak, and everyone listens. We use a talking piece, and when you have it, it's your time to share. When someone else has it, it's your time to listen. That respect for each other's voices is what makes this process work.
>
> What's great about responsive circles is that they're voluntary. You don't have to participate if you're not ready or comfortable, but if there's something on your mind, or if you want to resolve a conflict, this is a safe space to do it. You get to decide what you share and when you share it. No pressure. The point is to create understanding, to repair relationships, and to move forward in a positive way. In life, there are always going to be challenges, but it's how we handle those challenges that defines who we are. Responsive circles give you a chance to handle things in a way that builds respect, trust, and community.
>
> What do you think? Are you interested in circling up?

Figure 3.3: *High school–level responsive circle participation script.*
*Visit **go.SolutionTree.com/behavior** for a free reproducible version of this figure.*

These scripts are highly adaptable. You can edit them to fit a variety of settings and use them to encourage participation in a variety of contexts and situations. That being said, the facilitator has a few options if students who were harmed choose not to participate.

- **Allow more time to pass before facilitating the circle:** As they say, time heals all wounds. The student or students who were harmed may simply need a little more time before feeling comfortable circling up.
- **Circle up with only the student or students who caused the harm and focus on how their actions affected the class, the teacher, or the school community:** Many times, when students engage in conflict-inducing behavior, it impacts others in the school community.
- **Employ another corrective action that holds the student who committed the harm accountable:** This could include some type of reflection or written apology.

Most of the time, students are willing to participate.

Keep Families Informed

After conducting the initial investigation, the facilitator should speak with the family about the incident that occurred. In addition to sharing information about the incident, the facilitator informs parents of the plan to facilitate a responsive circle with all involved. The facilitator briefly explains the circle, including how the facilitator will help students process the conflict, decide how to repair any harm done, discuss ways to resolve the conflict and move on, and how to reintegrate students into the community. If the facilitator is not the administrator in charge of handling discipline, it may help to include the administrator in the conversation, as well.

Schedule the Meeting

One of the biggest challenges is that circles require lots of time. Administering traditional disciplinary measures like a detention is much quicker. That said, the time-intensive strengths of circles, including relationship building, reparation, conflict resolution, and reintegration, outweigh their time requirement drawbacks.

Identify a Safe, Private, and Comfortable Setting

It's evident when circling is part of the school culture and practice. In these schools, students feel comfortable sharing their thoughts, emotions, or concerns with the adults. Administrator offices aren't always the most trusting or comfortable places for circles. Sometimes, the social worker's office, a conference room, or an empty classroom might work best. The most important thing to consider is where students will feel safe and comfortable.

Choose a Number of Participants

Typically, circles include all individuals involved in a particular situation. However, taking this approach may cause circles to get too large. When the circle gets too large, and there are serious emotions involved, it may be hard to keep order and properly resolve the conflict. Nevertheless, circles usually work best with two or three participants, especially if it's a fairly serious conflict. The smaller the group, the more effective and efficient the resolution process. With that in mind, it's beneficial when the following individuals participate in responsive circles.

- **Individuals directly involved in the conflict:** Anyone who played a role in the incident or conflict, whether as an instigator or recipient, should be allowed to participate. This way, those involved can express their feelings, share their perspectives, and work together to resolve the issue.

- **Facilitator:** The facilitator, most often a teacher, social worker, or administrator, is essential for guiding the process, ensuring the circle follows a respectful and productive format, and helping participants stay on track during the discussion.

- **Peers or witnesses:** If others outside the direct conflict were affected or witnessed the incident, their inclusion could provide additional perspectives. Also, if applicable, this helps address and resolve the wider impact of a conflict.

- **Members of the school community:** In cases where the conflict has affected the broader school community, it may be appropriate to include other school members, such as additional staff, students, or even members of the outside community. As an example, if the issue centers on destruction of school property, the facilitator can include the custodial or maintenance staff usually responsible for caring for school property or community members living near the school. Like peers or witnesses, including members of the school community allows the wider impact of the situation to be addressed and resolved.

- **Other supportive adults:** At times, it may be appropriate to bring a trusted adult to the circle, such as a teacher or mentor, to help them feel supported throughout the process. For instance, when facilitating a circle with a student who has communication issues, it's helpful to include a member of that student's IEP team. When facilitating a circle with a student who is an English learner, for example, it's helpful to include another student or member of the English learning staff to help with translation.

Keep the circle relatively small (between three and five people) and ensure all participants agree to the norms of circle participation.

Determine Circle Structure

Facilitators will need to decide whether they will facilitate a sequential or nonsequential circle (page 73). Most of the time, responsive circles run best in nonsequential formats. This way, the conversation evolves organically as participants share their experiences and emotions. If or when facilitators attempt to regulate speech, emotions often become amplified. The choice between sequential and nonsequential structures really depends on the goals.

- **Sequential circles** are often preferred for creating a structured, predictable environment where everyone can be heard equally. That makes them ideal for community building or classroom discussions. What's more, this type of structure is helpful when a person is new to facilitating a circle or when facilitating a circle with less experienced participants (Isenberg, 2019; The Write of Your Life, n.d.).
- **Nonsequential circles** are more suitable for complex, emotionally charged situations, as they allow for a flexible flow of dialogue. At times, it can be a bit more challenging to maintain order and ensure participation in a nonsequential circle. For that reason, this structure is often more suitable for older, more experienced participants. Both structures have their strengths, and facilitators should choose based on the group's needs, age range, circle goal, and the nature of the issue being addressed (Isenberg, 2019; The Write of Your Life, n.d.).

Decide Whether and What Talking Piece to Use

Talking pieces can be very helpful when it comes to managing or encouraging speech in circles. They're often beneficial when circling with young students or with inexperienced participants. Using a talking piece may be a matter of personal preference. Some facilitators swear by them. Some prefer not to use them at all. Whether facilitators use a talking piece or not, all participants must stay focused and take the circle seriously.

Choose Norms

Similar to classroom expectations, norms help establish and ensure order, respect, and efficiency. Facilitators may create their own norms or create norms together with circle participants. Whatever the facilitators decide, norms are an important part of the circle process. The following norm examples are a good place to start. What's more, they are highly adaptable and can fit a variety of contexts and purposes.

- **Respect the talking piece:** The person holding the talking piece is the only one talking. This helps ensure everyone has an equal opportunity to share without interruption.
- **Listen with respect:** While someone else is speaking, participants should listen attentively without judgment or interruption. Listening deeply is key to understanding and building empathy.

- **Speak from the heart:** This norm encourages students to share thoughts and feelings openly and honestly. It helps call attention to the fact that circles are a safe space reserved for genuine expression.
- **Keep things confidential:** What's shared in circle stays in circle. Participants must feel that their personal stories and expressions will not be shared outside the group (unless there's a safety issue).
- **Pass if you need to:** Participants should have the freedom to pass if they're not comfortable or ready to share. Participation is highly encouraged but not forced. Participants must feel safe and comfortable before they can share.

Decide Roles

Facilitators should decide whether to include various roles based on several factors, including grade level or context, conflict complexity, group dynamics, and goals. What's more, there will be times when the facilitator can accomplish multiple roles simultaneously.

- **Facilitator:** Certain situations or contexts may require the facilitator to take a more active role. For instance, when facilitating responsive circles with elementary students, the facilitator may need to do more reminding regarding circle norms and encouraging regarding circle sharing. With older students or students who are more experienced with circles, the facilitator can usually take a less active role. However, circles are most effective and beneficial when the participants do the work and take ownership over the process. Also, while certain circles may require more input or involvement from the facilitator, the facilitator should refrain from passing judgment as much as possible. Stick with the facts, remain neutral as much as possible, and help the participants resolve their conflict. Facilitators may want to consider gender when facilitating circles. Some situations may be easier to resolve when the facilitator or co-facilitator are the same gender as their participants. It all depends on the situation.
- **Co-facilitator:** Co-facilitators support the facilitator by asking clarifying questions, helping students articulate their feelings, or taking notes. However, if the facilitator chooses to include a co-facilitator, they must both be on the same page regarding who's leading the circle, the circle process, and the goal of the circle.
- **Timekeeper:** Depending on the experience level of the facilitator or the severity of the conflict being addressed, the facilitator may also be able to serve as the timekeeper. Other times, the facilitator can appoint one of the circle participants as the timekeeper.
- **Normer, or circle guardian:** In some circles, it's helpful to have a participant who reminds other participants of the norms. In circles with older or more experienced participants, this role allows a participant to take

on some leadership responsibilities as they hold the rest of the participants responsible for observing circle norms. That being said, the normer, or circle guardian, should be experienced enough that reminding other participants of norms doesn't cause interruption or more conflict.

- **Note-taker:** At times, it can be helpful to identify a participant as the note-taker. Most of the time, the facilitator can accomplish this role (in addition to facilitating and timekeeping), especially if they're experienced. If the facilitator decides to identify a participant as a note-taker, this role should not interfere with the participant's participation in the circle.

After making these considerations and preparing, you will begin step one. The reproducible "Responsive Circle Steps" (page 65) lists the steps for easy reference.

Steps During the Responsive Circle

Most circle professional learning tends to be very philosophical and encourages trainees to develop systems or processes that work for them. For some, that may work. They may enjoy the autonomy and creativity in that. But that may also limit practicality, as it takes time for trainees to develop systems or processes that work for them. The point of this section is to make explicit the steps educators can follow to facilitate successful responsive circles. Consider this the blueprint for conducting successful responsive circles. This blueprint allows educators, whether they are teachers, social workers, guidance counselors, or administrators, to begin facilitating responsive circles immediately.

As mentioned, it's helpful when facilitators, especially those new to circles, start with something that has less at stake. Facilitating low-risk circles like learning and fishbowl assessment circles helps facilitators build confidence and refine their skills in a more controlled and less emotionally charged environment. They learn important skills such as guiding or encouraging conversation, managing norms, fostering trust, and managing group dynamics.

Please note that the post-circle debrief isn't listed as an official step, as it isn't always related or necessary for successful conflict resolution; however, it is important for continued support and communication. For instance, during post-circle check-ins, a facilitator or other circle participants can help monitor progress, uphold students' collective commitments, reinforce positive behavior, strengthen relationships, and provide emotional support.

These are the five steps to follow.

1. Analyze the harm.
2. Repair the harm.
3. Prevent future harm.
4. Make collective commitments.
5. Reintegrate.

Again, these steps are clearly delineated to help educators hone their craft as circle facilitators. Though it's recommended to practice facilitating with low-risk circles, educators could begin using this process and the stages starting tomorrow if they wanted to do so.

Step One: Analyze the Harm

During the first step, analyze the harm, circle participants focus on the harm that occurred during a particular incident. Participants, with some guidance and simple questioning from the facilitator, discuss what happened to process the conflict.

As facilitator, rely on your investigation notes to begin the facilitation process. If you're using a nonsequential format, you might simply ask, "What happened?" Because I have my notes available, I usually already know the answer to this question. But, hearing it directly from participants in the circle is essential for analysis and resolution.

Most of the time, in the elementary context, this simple question prompts an immediate response from someone in the circle. Be prepared. The first response often tends to be very accusatory: "Johnny did this to me at recess!" or "Michelle did that to me while in line!" Then, the expected rebuttal occurs, which includes some form of denial or another accusation. At the middle or secondary levels, the facilitator may need to be more tactful to get participants to begin discussing what happened. Facilitators can start by reminding participants in a calm and supportive tone that discussing conflict can be uncomfortable: "I know this might feel tough or uncomfortable, but talking about what happened can help us all feel better and move forward in a productive way." Then, facilitators can ask open-ended questions to all participants, such as, "Can anyone share what happened from your perspective?" or "Can someone share what you think led up to this situation?" These types of questions often elicit responses from someone.

If participants begin by accusing others in the circle, you can raise your hand to signal for attention and remind participants to simply recall the facts as they happened. I restate the question with something like, "What happened, and from the beginning." Interestingly, this inquiry accomplishes a few things: it helps refocus the circle, establishes a less accusatory tone, and helps participants dig a little deeper into the incident.

If for some reason these prompts don't elicit an immediate response, or even a somewhat delayed response, you might try a different approach. If participants are reluctant to participate, addressing one of them directly usually helps get the ball rolling. For example, you could say something like, "Johnny, do you know why we're here today?"

If there's too much talking at this point, you can refer to a norm regarding taking turns or not interrupting. If there's a talking piece (page 76) in play, the facilitator can remind circle participants that only the person with the piece is talking.

Once the conversation starts flowing, use the reproducible "Responsive Circle Notes" (page 66) to record important points and keep track of the conversation. You may have to cross-reference the notes form and your investigation notes. Do not take circle time to clarify investigation and circle note discrepancies. It's important for the participants to share their thoughts and feelings without interruption. Having all circle notes in a separate place (separate from investigation notes) may or may not be helpful to you.

Although I personally don't use a script, I do think scripts can be helpful, especially for those just starting out or for those who are still uncomfortable with the process. Whether the facilitator uses a script or not, questions like the ones listed in figure 3.4 help all participants analyze the harm that occurred during the incident. The last three questions focus specifically on empathy development. Specific questions geared toward putting students in others' perspectives are the tools facilitators use to transport students into the consciousness of their classmates or members of the school community.

What happened?

What was your part in the problem?

Why did this happen? Why do you think this happened?

Why did you engage in the behavior you did?

How did this make you feel?

How would you feel if something like this happened to you?

What impact has your behavior had on you, others, and your community?

How would it make you feel if this happened to you, and Bobby apologized to make it better?

If you were the person hurt in this situation, how would you want it to be fixed?

Figure 3.4: *Analyze the harm script.*

*Visit **go.SolutionTree.com/behavior** for a free reproducible version of this figure.*

Allow students to experience and share the feelings of another. In addition to these empathic questions, facilitators use affective statements to paint a vivid picture of how someone's actions harm another or a community. Statements like "It made me feel sad, scared, and unsafe when you stole my iPad" or "When you spray painted the gym, it made me feel angry, upset, and disappointed" disclose feelings that have a powerful impact. I've never had more success at developing empathy than with perspective-taking questions and affective communication deployed during the responsive circle process. It's powerful!

These question prompts help participants get a better picture of what transpired, why it may have happened, how it happened, and how it made all parties feel. Once participants have fleshed out important details while analyzing the harm, you can move into the next step.

Step Two: Repair the Harm

During the second step, repair the harm, participants discuss ways to repair harm done to a person, a place or thing, or the entire school community. Most of the time, the focus of this stage is on repairing harm done to another student. However, it can also apply when someone has damaged school property and harmed the entire school community as a result.

For example, I facilitated a circle with two seventh-grade students (who we'll call Dean and Justin) after they completely destroyed a student bathroom. They clogged all the drains, urinals, and stall toilets with toilet paper. By clogging all the drains with toilet paper, they caused severe flooding. What's more, they threw wet toilet paper all over the ceiling, over the stall railings, on the walls, and they stuck it to every mirror in the bathroom. When my custodian saw the mess and came to report it to me, he was visibly distraught. Because of their actions, that bathroom had to be closed for a portion of the day while the mess was cleaned. This required other students in this wing of the building to go up a flight of stairs to the second floor in order to use the bathroom.

After the students agreed to participate in a circle with each other, I also decided to invite our custodian and a few inconvenienced classmates. In the circle, we focused on how their actions hurt the custodian's feelings, made his job harder, and how they inconvenienced an entire wing of the building. Our custodian, who had previously never participated in something like this, really opened up about how he was so disappointed in the students because he'd never seen them do something like this before. The inconvenienced classmates shared how they were losing out on valuable learning and socializing time in their classroom because they had to walk up a flight of stairs to use the bathroom on another floor of the building. These testimonials really opened Dean's and Justin's eyes to the harm they'd done to our school and the people within it. Because of these testimonies, the boys felt horrible and were so ashamed.

Not only is this stage beneficial for the parties involved, but it can also be very rewarding for the facilitator. I often open this stage with a question like, "What can you do to fix this?" Many times, students are shocked I'm even seeking their input after they've engaged in conflict-inducing behavior. I've lost track of how many times students respond with something along the lines of, "I should serve a detention," "I should miss recess," "You should take away my free time," or, "I should go to ISS." Responses like these demonstrate how familiar students are with traditional disciplinary measures and punishments. Because this process is new for many students, it can be confusing. I clarify that I'm not asking for a type of punishment. Even after clarifying, students still have difficulty with this part of the process. It's the facilitator's job to get students to dig deeper and to think about ways to truly hold themselves responsible for their behavior.

Encourage participants to think about the situation from the perspective of the person who's been harmed. This perspective taking is extremely powerful and *always* elicits a groan or look of shame from the participant who engaged in the conflict-inducing behavior (Making Caring Common Project, n.d.). When the facilitator encourages perspective taking, this helps students develop empathy and realize they have a responsibility to be helpful and supportive members of their community. After asking the boys to think about the situation from Mr. Jack's perspective, they started discussing how this incident would make them feel if they were Mr. Jack. Dean even answered, "I would be so angry if some kids did this, and I had to clean all this up!"

When students begin to empathize with those they've harmed, they truly begin to think about ways of holding themselves responsible for their actions. Participants may start generating their own ideas about how they could repair the harm they've caused. For example, Dean said they could clean the bathroom. Before we even convened the circle, I knew I wanted them to arrive at this conclusion, but I wanted them to arrive at this suggestion on their own. By doing so, they took more ownership over the harm they caused and the process of repairing it than if I had come right out with this consequence.

It's more powerful when participants develop ideas and suggestions for making things right themselves. When students are empowered to take responsibility for their actions and contribute to the resolution, it fosters deeper reflection, accountability, and a stronger sense of empathy; these are essential for long-term behavior change and conflict resolution (Darling-Hammond, 2023). After going through the rest of the stages in the responsive circle process, Dean and Justin helped Mr. Jack clean the bathroom (with parent permission). A byproduct of repairing harm is relationship mending or relationship building. In this instance, after empathizing with Mr. Jack and helping him clean the bathroom, the boys developed a very strong relationship with him. From then on, Mr. Jack checked up on the boys, talking to their teachers and their parents about them. Dean and Justin grew to love Mr. Jack, and he loved them right back.

There are a variety of ways students can repair harm.

- Apologize verbally or in writing
- Offer a physical gesture like a handshake or a hug (the recipient, of course, must consent to accept this without any pressure to do so)
- Clean a mess they've made
- Pay for something they've purposefully damaged or stolen

Regardless of what a participant suggests, it is essential to empathize with those they have harmed, generate their own ideas for repairing the harm, and then accomplish those things. That being said, if participants are reluctant to offer suggestions for how they can repair the harm they caused, the facilitator could offer some gentle suggestions or possibilities to get them started. For example, facilitators could say, "Some people in similar situations have apologized, repaired something that was broken, helped a participant with a task, or helped clean a mess they made." Offering a range of ideas like this gives students direction without making them feel pressured.

Apologies can be a good place to start. But, in addition to an apology, participants who've committed harm should also engage in some type of corrective action to make amends. For example, if a participant has committed harm and is now apologizing, as the facilitator, you might say, "Thank you for your apology. That's a good start. What else can you do to help make things right?" This prompting gets participants to think a little deeper about how they can make amends.

It should be noted that apologies are very complex. Genuine apologies play an important role in conflict resolution, but their effectiveness depends heavily on the sincerity and understanding of the harm caused and when students choose to apologize on their own terms (Payne & Welch, 2022). What's more, while apologies can help rebuild relationships, foster empathy, and promote accountability, they are most impactful when they're accompanied by actions that show a commitment to repairing harm (McCluskey, 2018). Be careful, though. Apologies can make situations worse, especially if those who've been harmed aren't ready or are unwilling to accept the apology (Costello et al., 2019). What's more, many participants who have been harmed need more than a verbal apology to repair the harm done.

During the repair the harm stage, the questions in figure 3.5 can be extremely helpful in terms of getting students to begin communicating in the circle.

How can this be repaired?

What can you do to fix this?

What do you think needs to happen to make things right?

What needs to happen to make things better?

How do you think you can demonstrate that you're sorry?

If this were you, what would you want done to make it better?

Figure 3.5: *Repair the harm script.*

Visit go.SolutionTree.com/behavior for a free reproducible version of this figure.

Step Three: Prevent Future Harm

The third stage, prevent future harm, is all about brainstorming ways to prevent the same or similar conflict from happening again. During prevent future harm, the facilitator assists students as they generate potential solutions for avoiding the same kind of conflict-inducing behavior in the future. Like most stages in the responsive circle process, preventing future harm is most effective when students do the work themselves. Not only should students generate ideas for preventing future harm, but they should also be able to explain why their ideas would be helpful in preventing future conflict. Examples follow.

- **Immediately seek adult support:** In conflict situations, students often act impulsively by taking matters into their own hands. For example, name-calling and hitting may result in the person being hit or called names retaliating in kind. Instead of retaliating during conflict situations, students should immediately seek the help and support of a trusted or nearby adult.

- **Engage in mindfulness strategies:** Similarly, rather than acting impulsively and immediately retaliating in a conflict situation, students can do breathing exercises (such as box breathing). Strategies like this can help prevent conflict or prevent conflict from escalating.

Again, students must do the heavy lifting. If done well, the conversation in this stage usually leads seamlessly into the fourth step called make collective commitments.

After brainstorming ideas for preventing future harm, lead the circle into a conversation about what will happen if participants can't prevent this same conflict from occurring again. Discuss how you really don't like issuing punishments, emphasizing how you would much rather help students resolve their conflicts in circle settings instead of simply issuing punishments. But explain that if this conflict happens again, even after reaching resolution, you will be forced to no longer focus on relationships or repair but rather on discipline.

At this point, you can review the discipline detour, which is a hybrid of restorative practices and a progressive discipline system. The path is contextual and adaptable. It should fit your setting. Keep in mind that research indicates that a juvenile knowing they will be punished for behavior can deter negative behaviors, but making discipline more severe doesn't help deter someone (Loughran et al., 2015).

If the same conflict exists after the responsive circle process, the discipline detour, regardless of student age or context, can include the following actions in the given order. This is not unlike many existing school discipline plans, and that is why it is a last resort.

1. **Immediate family or guardian notification:** Immediately notify the parent or guardian of the issue. Remind the parent that you already facilitated a responsive circle with all involved in hopes of successfully resolving the conflict and moving forward. Explain that, unfortunately, the conflict persists, and the student has chosen another direction. It may be necessary to require a mandatory parent meeting where the student and their family or guardian discuss the persistent issue with the administrator responsible for discipline. Inform the adults that if the behavior persists even after the meeting, the school will be forced to engage the next step of the discipline detour.

2. **Lunch reflection and family or guardian notification:** If the same behavior or conflict continues, the administrator can issue what some call a *reflection*. Students meet with an administrator or other staff member (preferably during lunch) to engage in reflection activities (journaling, writing to prompts, graphic organizers, and the like). The punitive aspect of this measure, students missing out on eating lunch with their friends, can help rectify some situations, especially for elementary students.

3. **Detention and family or guardian notification:** Again, if the same behavior or conflict persists, the administrator can administer a before-school or after-school detention. Administrators must notify the family or guardian.

4. **In-school suspension and family or guardian notification:** If the behavior or conflict continues, the administrator can administer an in-school suspension. Administrators must notify the family or guardian.

5. **Out-of-school suspension and family or guardian notification:** If the behavior or conflict continues, the administrator can administer an out-of-school suspension. Administrators must notify family or guardian.

Principals and other administrators can employ the discipline detour if restorative approaches don't work, but keep in mind it is reserved for the administrator responsible for administering discipline. This way, the classroom teacher remains restorative, with a focus on building and sustaining relationships. Teachers have their classroom management plans, which include clearly established expectations, rules, procedures, routines, and some type of corrective action.

The hope is that, when offered the choice between the responsive circle process and the discipline detour, students will choose the circle process. In my experience and context, the detour is extremely rare. Students choose the responsive circle process almost all the time. I've seen successful circles work with and without the inclusion of aspects of progressive discipline systems. However, after years of practice and experience, the reproducible "Discipline Detour" (page 67) may help foster prevention for certain students.

Like other stages, preventing future harm can help you simultaneously teach life skills, especially some important and useful coping or redirection strategies (Hannigan & Hannigan, 2024). For instance, you might touch on strategies like the following during circles.

- *Zones of regulation* is a framework for helping students develop control and emotional self-regulation (Zones of Regulation, n.d.). Feelings are divided into four color-coded zones. Based on the feeling and the zone, there are certain strategies students can use to help gain a sense of control. The zones of regulation are a schoolwide resource in my school, and multiple educators throughout the building use them. Because they're so ubiquitous, when I touch on this approach during a circle, for students, it's like a review.

- *Size of the problem* has participants divide problems into three categories: (1) small, (2) medium, and (3) large. Students can try strategies paired with the problem size for themselves or to support someone else (Beck, 2024). Examples follow.

  - *Small*—These are minor problems that can be independently managed. Examples are things such as losing a pencil, not liking what is for lunch, being embarrassed because you didn't know an answer when called on, or not being picked for a game. Students make a plan, engage in some breathing exercises (see the reproducible "Mindfulness Exercises," page 68), or ask a friend for help.
  - *Medium*—These are issues that may cause more significant frustration or inconvenience and require more time or effort to resolve. However, they are not emergencies, and the long-term impact is pretty minor. Examples include missing a homework deadline, arguing with a friend, or being late to school. Medium problems often require problem-solving skills and emotional regulation, but do not typically require adult support or result in severe or long-term consequences.
  - *Large*—These issues can have serious or long-lasting repercussions, may be difficult to solve, and often require adult support or intervention.

These problems can cause significant emotional distress and often cannot be resolved quickly. Examples include serious illness or injury, bullying or harassment, or parental divorce. These types of problems usually require significant support, whether from family members, educators, or external resources. Students experiencing these types of issues should immediately seek adult assistance.

This stage is a good opportunity to explicitly teach certain social-emotional skills. This is dramatically different from traditional disciplinary measures, where no teaching occurs.

The questions in figure 3.6 can help facilitate conversation during the prevent future harm step.

What can you do to make sure this doesn't happen again?

Next time, what can you do instead?

How will you respond if something similar happens in the future?

Figure 3.6: *Prevent future harm script.*

*Visit **go.SolutionTree.com/behavior** for a free reproducible version of this figure.*

As mentioned, typically, this stage leads right into the fourth stage of the responsive circle process referred to as make collective commitments.

Step Four: Make Collective Commitments

You may notice something interesting and powerful happen in this step. Students may not only help each other generate solutions, but they may also offer to support other circle participants as they work to implement their solutions. Here is an example from my work: I facilitated a circle with Kim and Shayna, two middle school students who'd been struggling with friend/not-friend drama. Kim explained how whenever she disagreed or didn't go along with something Shayna said, Shayna would tell her they were no longer friends. Kim described how this made her feel sad, and she would sometimes go along with whatever Shayna wanted just so they could remain friends.

As we made our way through analyzing the harm, Kim clearly articulated how Shayna's actions made her feel upset, mad, and alone. Shayna began to see how threatening to withhold friendship from someone could make that person feel. Moving into repairing the harm, Shayna apologized for her actions and clarified that she didn't want to hurt people's feelings, especially those of her friend Kim. In a shaky voice, she described how not getting things she wanted made her very angry, and sometimes, she couldn't control that anger. I vividly remember her saying how angry she would feel and how that showed up in her body.

The school's social worker and I then processed those emotions with Shayna, and I asked if there were any strategies she may have learned during the lesson that could help.

She thought for a long while. I was fighting the urge to interject when, finally, she said she realized that if someone disagreed with her, she could stop and think before reacting. She also said that she could use *I can* statements to share how it made her feel when she didn't get what she wanted.

Ms. Jessy smiled from ear to ear and commended Shayna for remembering strategies they talked about during the lesson. She also mentioned how happy she was that Shayna would be willing to try those strategies in an emotional situation. Then, seemingly out of nowhere, Kim excitedly exclaimed, "I'm really good at thinking before reacting. When I'm upset, I usually count to five before saying anything. I can help you with that if you want." Shayna agreed to receive the help.

How amazingly forgiving and resilient our students can be! Even after experiencing sadness and hurt, Kim was still willing to help Shayna be a better friend. When students help others fulfill their commitments, it fosters forgiveness and resolution, which both lead to prevention (Enright, 2022).

You may or may not want to prompt or guide students to help each other uphold their commitments. There will be times when one participant won't feel safe or comfortable helping the other. It is not their responsibility to offer that support. The person who committed the harm must take responsibility for their own actions and work for reparation and prevention, but it's not incumbent on the affected individual to accept reparations. That's a major part of the learning process. Nevertheless, if and when it does happen naturally, consider nurturing it.

You may want to have students sign the commitments. Regarding them signing: some say that signing off connotes a contract. Others say that signing off on something and then keeping it can serve as a painful reminder for the students involved. You can have students sign their agreement in circle with the reproducible "Collective Commitments Agreement" (page 69). There are no investigation notes or details on the form. It's extremely general, so it is safe for students to share. You may want to encourage students to show their parents or guardians for a discussion at home.

After signing, make a copy for all students involved. After participants have their own copy of the agreement, you can refer back to the agreement with students or use it as a physical reminder of the commitments made during circle. I have known students who taped their agreements inside their locker door to serve as a reminder. Once, while in the hallway, an elementary student pulled me aside to show me his agreement. Another kept his in his wallet as a reminder. What's more, the agreement serves as a reminder of the commitments made to others in circle. It's also a commitment to the notion that, as students uphold their commitments to each other, as they better themselves, they're bettering the entire school community.

Students can use the copy to measure progress if applicable. For example, a few weeks after the circle with Shayna and Kim, I saw Shayna in the lunchroom and referenced the agreement. I put it in front of us and asked how she was doing with thinking before reacting when she didn't get her way. She said that she'd been struggling but was trying very hard and hadn't threatened withholding friendship from anyone. She said she even asked Ms. Jessy to review the strategy during one of her sessions.

During the collective commitments step, the questions in figure 3.7 help students engage in productive and focused dialogue.

> How will you (or we) demonstrate that you (or we) are committed to making a change?
> How will you know if you've been successful?
> How will others know if you've been successful?
> What can you do to show that you're serious about resolving this conflict?

Figure 3.7: Collective commitments script.
Visit ***go.SolutionTree.com/behavior*** *for a free reproducible version of this figure.*

Step Five: Reintegrate

Reintegration helps students rejoin the community with minimal disruption after harming an individual or the entire school community. It's one of the most important aspects of the responsive circle process. But, as the last stage of the process, it's also the most overlooked and often forgotten stage. Facilitators feel that after reparations have been made and collective commitments have been agreed on and signed, the conflict is over. They think the conflict is completely resolved. Indeed, those stages are absolutely essential. Reparation and agreeing to uphold commitments help move the circle toward resolution.

Without reintegration, however, actual resolution is hard to achieve because participants, especially the ones who caused harm, may never obtain closure. The participants who caused harm and are working to make amends often need support in doing so. Reintegration offers facilitators an opportunity to check in with those participants and offer support as they work to uphold their commitments. What's more, cultivating a culture of prevention requires welcoming students back into the community. True resolution can only be achieved when those who've caused harm are welcomed back into the community as equals.

You do not need to facilitate reintegration during the actual circle process—especially not for more serious incidents. After more serious incidents, everyone involved may need more time to process what was discussed, reflect on the emotions that surfaced (see the reproducible "Responsive Circle Reflection," page 70), and internalize commitments. What's more, this gives adults, including teachers, social workers, guidance counselors, and administrators, a bit more time to monitor the situation. You can conclude the circle after signing off on collective commitments. In this case, a check-in can offer you and the students time to determine how to diplomatically and privately speak with the participants about moving forward.

I remember advising a middle school dean on a circle she wanted to facilitate with two sixth-grade boys. Connie, a middle school dean for two years, sent me an email about an incident. She explained that Matt and Javier, two competitive sixth-grade boys, were involved in a physical altercation during gym. After scoring a goal, Javier boasted about being a better player and made inappropriate comments about Matt. Matt became upset, lost his composure, and punched Javier. The teacher arrived immediately and stopped the altercation from escalating. Both boys were escorted to Connie's office. Connie said immediately facilitating a circle was out of the question because the boys were still angry. Nevertheless, Connie wanted their parents to be aware of the situation and to discuss her intention to facilitate a circle once the students calmed down. While speaking to their parents, she mentioned that if the boys couldn't regain composure and agree to a circle that afternoon, she'd call the boys out of class the next day to facilitate the circle. She did clarify for all parents that there might be other discipline, depending on her investigation and the circle outcome. Physical altercations like this were not allowed at school. She ended by stating she was hopeful that she could help the boys resolve the conflict and prevent future issues.

Connie shared that Matt's parents were open to the circle, but the superintendent contacted her after hearing about the altercation through Javier's father. Javier's dad opposed the circle and wanted a more severe consequence for the other boy, such as a suspension. Now, Connie was torn between using a circle or issuing a different discipline. I reminded Connie that while we may disagree with the use of certain traditional disciplinary measures, she could combine them with a responsive circle. I also reminded her that if using a traditional disciplinary measure like a suspension, it's essential to facilitate reintegration. After discussing it, Connie decided to combine approaches: facilitate a responsive circle with the boys, issue Matt the suspension, and reintegrate Matt when he returned to school.

Two weeks later, I received a follow-up email from an excited Connie. She felt good about the circle, but felt best about the reintegration. She had brought together Matt, Javier, and the gym teacher. She mentioned that though she didn't think Matt and Javier would be friends, they would respect each other moving forward. I agreed that we can't force participants to be friends with each other and that respecting each other is a step in the right direction.

Reintegration is important for the following reasons (Morgan et al., 2014).

- Setting expectations for moving forward
- Offering participants further opportunity to accept responsibility for their actions
- Introducing participants back into the community
- Discussing necessary support participants may need while striving to meet their collective commitments

Reintegration, for the most part, takes time when educators are already extraordinarily busy, but it's pivotal to the process. Don't omit this step despite being already pressed for time, even if it feels like everything is resolved and it's time to move on.

The questions in figure 3.8 (page 58) can help facilitate conversation prior to and during reintegration.

> Can you share how you've been feeling since the incident happened?
>
> What did you learn from your time away?
>
> Are there specific actions you think would help rebuild trust with your classmates or teachers?
>
> What are your expectations moving forward?
>
> What support do you think you need to help you stick to your collective commitments?
>
> Is there anything else you'd like to share before we close? What positive things do you hope will come out of this process?

Figure 3.8: Reintegration script.

*Visit **go.SolutionTree.com/behavior** for a free reproducible version of this figure.*

Post-Circle Debrief

After a conflict has been successfully resolved, it's important that all parties move forward productively. That's not saying everyone forgets what happened. That would be impossible, especially if it's a fairly serious incident. However, the expectation is that all parties move forward after committing to repair harm, learn from mistakes, and work to become better versions of themselves. That being said, it's important to be realistic about relationships. Educators using circles should understand that not everyone will be friends, even after successfully repairing harm and resolving a conflict. That's OK. You can remind students throughout the process that they are not required to be friends. They do, however, need to respect each other and use the strategies they have learned to prevent the situation from occurring again.

Debriefing after a responsive circle involves the facilitator sharing information with important members of the circle or school community members, including teachers, a student's support or special education team, other staff as necessary, student participants, and student families. It includes reflecting on the circle's outcomes, assessing its effectiveness, addressing any unresolved issues, and keeping members of the school community informed. Debriefing allows members of the school community to process the experience, discuss the emotional impact, and identify what went well and what could be improved. The next sections explain more about what an administrator facilitator-to-staff, teacher facilitator-to-staff, administrator- or teacher-to-student, and administrator- or teacher-to-family debrief should include.

Administrator Facilitator-to-Staff

If the administrator facilitates the responsive circle between students, it's essential to keep members of the school community informed—especially the students' teachers. Naturally, teachers will have questions about the consequences students receive. Also, this is an opportunity to mention any adult supports the students may need to uphold their commitments and prevent a similar conflict.

If the incident was particularly egregious, it's also important to inform the entire building staff. For instance, an entire staff are part of addressing large fights that cause a sizable disruption. An administrator facilitator can communicate a variety of ways.

- **Staff communication:** The administrator facilitator can send an all-staff communiqué regarding the incident. If sending this kind of communication, the administrator facilitator must stick to the facts. In fact, it's helpful to divide the communiqué into bullets that include who, what, where, when, why, and how. Individually addressing these bullets in a communiqué can help structure and communicate only the essential information. Obviously, it's important the administrator facilitator remove any identifiable information, including student names. It's possible to communicate the necessary information without including specific identifiable information.

- **Individual conversations with those closest to the incident:** One-to-one conversations and a staff meeting (next bullet) usually go together. This is the staff debrief process I usually adhere to because it allows me to address those closest to the issue in a timely fashion and then follow up with the rest of the staff. The facilitator briefly mentions the following.
  - Conflict details
  - How the circle transpired
  - Whether family was informed
  - What the participants' collective commitments are
  - Additional disciplinary measures administered
  - Any supports the students need to uphold commitments

  It works in all contexts as well, including elementary and secondary schools.
  - *Elementary*—The facilitator speaks directly with the teacher of each student involved in the conflict, sticking to the who, what, where, when, why, and how.
  - *Middle and high school*—The facilitator speaks directly with the homeroom teachers or each student involved in the conflict. In this setting, if the conflict was large and witnessed by many staff members, those staff members are also addressed.

- **Staff meeting update:** After speaking individually with team members closest to the incident, the facilitator can address the rest of the staff during a faculty meeting. Some facilitators host voluntary after- or before-school meetings to debrief; some address the incident during a preexisting monthly faculty meeting. This way, those closest to the incident, who are the priority, are informed directly, while other members of the school community are informed later.

The template in figure 3.9 can help facilitate written and face-to-face conversations during post-circle debrief.

> **Who:** Who was involved? If communicating in writing, be very general. *Do not mention student names!* It is inadvisable to even use initials.
>
> **What:** What actually transpired? Was it a fight? Was it a verbal argument? Was it an issue over social media?
>
> **Where:** Where did the conflict occur?
>
> **When:** When did the conflict occur?
>
> **Why:** Why did the conflict occur? What did the facilitator's investigation notes reveal? What did circle participants say during circle?
>
> **How:** How was the conflict resolved? What commitments will the students uphold? Was any other discipline administered?

Figure 3.9: Administrator facilitator debrief script.

*Visit **go.SolutionTree.com/behavior** for a free reproducible version of this figure.*

Teacher Facilitator-to-Staff

When a teacher facilitates a circle in their classroom, it's essential to communicate about the incident and its resolution to the following people, for various reasons.

- **Any other staff witnesses or educators to whom the students are connected:** For example, students might have different classroom teachers, and all of them need to know what occurred.
- **Building leader:** If the same conflict occurs again, the administrator responsible for administering discipline may need to get involved.
- **Families or guardians:** As mentioned elsewhere, it is critical *not* to share specific information about any students other than the child of the parent being informed.

Teacher facilitators can use the administrator facilitator debrief script in figure 3.9 or adapt it in a way that works for them. However, just like written debriefs from administrator facilitators, the teacher facilitator must stick to the facts and not include any information identifying a student.

Administrator- or Teacher-to-Student

Outside of the official five-step process for facilitating responsive circles, check-ins can be extremely helpful in cultivating prevention. After facilitating a circle with a group of students and going through each individual stage of the process, it's always beneficial to follow up with them about the progress they're making toward their commitments. These check-ins show students that I still care and they should, too. In a way, they also show that I'm still paying attention to what's going on and that I can provide additional support if they want or need it.

Check-ins can be brief and informal. Typically, the first few days after the circle is the best time to facilitate a check-in with a student. Facilitators can use the processes in table 3.1 for checking in with students.

Table 3.1: Checking In After a Circle

WHEN	One to three days after circle	After significant milestones
PURPOSE	This is an optimal time to check in to see how students are doing and to ensure they are still on track with their commitments.	If the circle involved commitments with deadlines, such as an apology, written reflection, a behavior change, or some kind of restitution, checking in after one of these milestones shows students and families that the facilitator cares about the progress circle participants are making. It's the perfect opportunity to celebrate success with the students upholding their commitments.
FOCUS	These early check-ins allow the facilitator to gauge whether students need any additional support to reinforce accountability and closure. It's also an opportune time to ensure tensions have not resurfaced and students feel comfortable following through with their commitments.	This check-in helps participants feel successful while fulfilling their commitments. It's also an opportunity to gauge whether the participant needs further support.

While checking in, the questions in figure 3.10 will help students reflect, take accountability, and process their emotions, and offer an opportunity for the student to ask for additional support.

Have you had the chance to reflect on the responsive circle you participated in?

How is progress going toward resolution, forgiveness, or upholding your collective commitments?

Has the situation we sought to resolve continued or happened again?

Figure 3.10: Administrator or teacher facilitator-to-student script.
Visit **go.SolutionTree.com/behavior** *for a free reproducible version of this figure.*

Depending on the student or the situation, a more formal check-in may be advised. The goal is still the same: to follow up and provide extra support if necessary. However, consider talking to the student privately to focus more on the conversation. Then, if added as part of the student's intervention plan, document the conversation in your school's intervention database. For the students who have these formal check-ins as part of their intervention plans, it's even more important they occur consistently.

In addition to reintegrating students, it's also helpful to involve them in the community. Getting students involved in school helps cultivate a positive and preventive culture. Getting involved in school is good for relationships, it's good for academics, it's good for social development, and it's good for expanding skills like problem solving and collaboration (Center for Responsive Schools, n.d.; Gonser, 2021). It's good all around! Your school may not have many club or after-school activity options, which makes finding ways to involve students a little tricky. If that is the case, consider what roles and responsibilities students could have in the classroom and the rest of the building.

One student I knew had been in a fight. After Tony participated in a responsive circle focused on fighting, his fighting stopped. But, a few weeks later, Tony was in trouble for a different behavior. We did a responsive circle on name-calling and making others feel sad. That behavior stopped. Again, a few weeks later, Tony was in trouble for a new and different behavior. We did a responsive circle on the behavior, and it stopped. This continued with replacement behaviors, so I consulted with his teacher.

His classroom teacher said she noticed Tony taking on more leadership roles and responsibilities in the classroom. Tony's excitement started over small roles, like line leader and supply retriever, and then led to roles with more responsibility, such as a lunch and recess monitor and a small group captain. I realized he could be given responsibilities that echoed schoolwide. For instance, I talked to him about showing responsibility on the bus and how he could eventually serve as a bus monitor. I clearly explained what the role entailed and how he would know if he was a successful bus monitor. Every day, he asked when he could get started. Eventually, Tony was ready for the bus role. He obviously took immense pride in these roles, giving me daily updates about the happenings on the bus! I noticed how seriously he took his responsibilities and the effort he put forth to maintain those roles. He still made mistakes, even while engaged in his jobs. His family even noticed a difference.

The questions in figure 3.11 can help facilitate written and face-to-face conversations during post-circle debrief.

How have you been feeling since the circle? Is there anything you'd like to share?

Do you think you've been able to follow through on the commitments you made?

Are there any barriers making it hard for you to stick to your commitments?

What other support would you like to help you uphold your commitments?

How do you feel your relationships with others in the circle have been since the discussion?

Do you think the conflict has been resolved, or are there any lingering feelings or concerns?

Figure 3.11: *Facilitator formal check-in script.*

*Visit **go.SolutionTree.com/behavior** for a free reproducible version of this figure.*

Administrator- or Teacher-to-Family

After facilitating a circle, I always follow up with parents. In my experience, making a phone call to debrief with parents is the best way to keep them informed. With phone calls, there's less room for misinterpretation. I'm sure to be very clear about the who, what, where, when, why, and how. Also, when debriefing with families and guardians, focus only on *their* child. As you likely know, discussing other students is usually against district policy and certainly is a privacy issue; discuss nothing related to other students during your debrief with a family or guardian. Many times, that's easier said than done, as the adults often have questions about the consequences other children will receive. Even when that happens, keep the focus on their child and their child alone.

The script in figure 3.12 helps with this kind of debrief conversation over the phone.

Make clear the following in succinct terms.

Who: Who was involved? When speaking with parents, you can mention that another child was involved in the conflict. You can also discuss other staff members who may have been involved. But, as stated, do not discuss or mention any other children specifically. Keep information about other children limited and extremely general.

What: What actually transpired? Was it a fight? Was it a verbal argument? Was it an issue over social media?

Where: Where did the conflict occur?

When: When did the conflict occur?

Why: Why did the conflict occur? What did the facilitator's investigation notes reveal? What did circle participants say about precipitating factors? Again, keep information about other children limited and extremely general.

How: How was the conflict resolved? What commitments will this parent's child uphold? Will this specific child require any additional supports to uphold the commitments? Was there any other discipline (punishments) administered to this specific child?

If the parent inquires about other children involved, state the following.

I'm not at liberty to discuss other students. I am calling to debrief with you about your child and focus on how we will help them through this conflict.

Figure 3.12: *Family or guardian phone call debrief script.*
Visit **go.SolutionTree.com/behavior** *for a free reproducible version of this figure.*

In this chapter, I outlined a comprehensive blueprint of the responsive circle process, from preparation to reintegration and debrief. Each stage offers a structured approach to resolving conflict, promoting empathy, and fostering accountability for circle participants. The included scripts serve as practical tools to guide facilitators through various stages, ensuring conversations remain focused, respectful, and productive. As you move forward, these scripts will help you feel confident in navigating the complexities.

Either with your team or on your own, respond to the discussion questions and consider what next steps to take with the following guidance.

DISCUSSION QUESTIONS

Imagine you're leading your first responsive circle. What structure or format would you use? Would you utilize any circle facilitation tools? If so, which ones and why?

Suppose you must facilitate a digital circle. How would you structure the digital circle? Would you use any circle facilitation tools? Why or why not?

Suppose a student in your responsive circle is reluctant to participate. Maybe they're nervous. Maybe they're scared. Maybe they're struggling with answering the questions you're posing. What are some strategies you can deploy to help participants join the conversation and recall the facts of an incident?

Imagine facilitating a circle with primary students. They're eager to participate, but you feel like some of the things you're talking about may be over their heads. How can you modify or adapt the responsive circle process so younger students can participate?

NEXT STEPS

Experiment with circle variations. Explore different types of circles, such as learning and fishbowl, to see how they work, gauge how students respond to them, and build facilitation confidence.

Talk with successful facilitators. Reach out to educators who have successfully facilitated responsive circles in their schools. Interview them to talk about how they got started, what went well, what didn't, and any additional institutional knowledge.

Create a facilitator tool kit. Assemble a tool kit that includes scripts, questions, and prompts for various stages of the responsive circle process. Include supplies and materials like a talking piece, note-taking templates, and a list of restorative questions.

Responsive Circle Steps

These are the five steps to a responsive circle.

Step 1: Analyze the Harm

What happened? What was your part in the problem? What impact has your behavior had on you, others, or the school community? How do you feel when you get teased or hit, or have something stolen?

Step 2: Repair the Harm

What can you do to fix this? What do you think needs to happen in order to make things right? How can this be repaired? How do you think you could demonstrate that you're sorry?

Step 3: Prevent Future Harm

What can you do to make sure this doesn't happen again? Next time, what can you do instead? How will you respond if something similar happens in the future? Preview the discipline detour.

Step 4: Make Collective Commitments

How will we demonstrate we're committed to making a change? How will I or you know if I'm successful? What can I do to show I'm serious about resolving this conflict?

Step 5: Reintegrate

Reintegrate students into the classroom or school environment. Try welcoming them back with a circle or morning meeting. Review commitments and expectations for moving forward.

Responsive Circle Notes

Date:

ANALYZE THE HARM

REPAIR THE HARM

PREVENT FUTURE HARM

COLLECTIVE COMMITMENTS

REINTEGRATION OR FOLLOW-UP

Discipline Detour

Name: Class:

Issue:

STEP ONE: CIRCLE

STEP TWO: REFLECTION

STEP THREE: DETENTION

STEP FOUR: IN-SCHOOL SUSPENSION OR OUT-OF-SCHOOL SUSPENSION

Mindfulness Exercises

These are different breathing exercises that can help improve your mindfulness. You can close your eyes while you do the breathing exercises, or simply look down, to help focus.

Box Breathing

Box breathing focuses on counts of four, like the sides of a box.

1. Breathe in slowly through your nose as you silently count to four. Focus on feeling the air go into your lungs.
2. Hold your breath and silently count to four.
3. Slowly breathe out, through your mouth, and silently count to four.
4. Hold and silently count to four.
5. Repeat until you feel calmer.

Balanced Breathing

Balanced breathing focuses on breathing from your diaphragm. Throughout the exercise, your right hand—on your chest—should not move up and down as you inhale and exhale. If it does, use your diaphragm (or "stomach") instead. When you do that, you'll notice your stomach moving as you inhale and exhale.

1. Sit tall, with your spine straight, but not rigid. Your chin should be parallel to the floor.
2. Put your left hand on your stomach, and your right hand on your chest.
3. Breathe in slowly through your nose and silently count to four. Notice your left hand and belly go up.
4. Slowly breathe out, through your mouth, and silently count to four. Notice your left hand and belly go down.
5. Do this three or four times. If you practice consistently, go up to ten breaths.

Balloon Belly Breathing

Balloon belly breathing focuses on feeling, internally and externally, the sensation of your stomach moving as you breathe.

1. Put your hands on your stomach.
2. Breathe slowly in through your nose. Feel your stomach expand like it is an inflating balloon.
3. Count silently to four.
4. Slowly breathe out through your mouth for four seconds. Feel your stomach deflate, like a balloon with the air let out.
5. Repeat until you feel calmer.

Five Senses

This exercise requires you to draw your attention away from your emotions and notice your surroundings and name them.

1. Name five things you can see.
2. Name four things you can feel.
3. Name three things you can hear.
4. Name two things you can smell.
5. Name one thing you can taste.

Source: Hierck, T., & Weber, C. (2024). Positive behaviors start with positive mindsets: Twenty-eight actions to motivate students and boost achievement. Solution Tree Press.

Collective Commitments Agreement

COMMITMENT	RATIONALE OR REASON

Name: _____ Initials: _____

Name: _____ Initials: _____

Name: _____ Initials: _____

Date: _____

Responsive Circles © 2025 Solution Tree Press • SolutionTree.com
Visit **go.SolutionTree.com/behavior** to download this free reproducible.

Responsive Circle Reflection

Date:

 WHAT HAPPENED?

 WHAT COULD YOU HAVE DONE DIFFERENTLY?

 WHO DID YOUR BEHAVIOR AFFECT?

 HOW WILL YOU REPAIR THE HARM?

HOW DID IT MAKE YOU FEEL?

HOW ARE YOU MEETING YOUR COLLECTIVE COMMITMENTS?

Responsive Circles © 2025 Solution Tree Press • SolutionTree.com
Visit **go.SolutionTree.com/behavior** to download this free reproducible.

CHAPTER 4

Circle Types and Tools

I'd been up since the crack of dawn revising my presentation. I was presenting a workshop for administrators and teacher leaders that day. Later that morning, participants arrived and walked to open desks, which were organized in rows. I thought little of it as I made my way around the room greeting people. Finally, I stood at the front of the room and began. The energy was high. The vibes were good. Everyone was engaged and welcoming. As I began to feel more comfortable, I moved between rows to get a better glimpse of participants; it had been tough to establish connections with them, and I was trying to figure out why.

During our introductions, one of the more vocal teacher leaders welcomed me to the district. While participants briefly shared their experiences and understandings of restorative practices, this participant turned around to make eye contact with others as they shared. After a while, she stopped turning around to see her colleagues. There was a change in her energy.

As everyone returned from lunch, I asked participants to move all the desks to the back of the room. We kept our chairs and reorganized ourselves into a big circle around the room. In this setup, it was much easier to see and hear each other. After shifting things about, as we found different places to sit, I saw the aforementioned participant hugging a colleague before sitting down. Seeing her reengaged and reenergized felt good. And it wasn't just her energy that shifted. The entire dynamic changed. People who hadn't participated yet began speaking up. The rate and depth of participation increased. It felt like we trusted each other more and like an opportunity for collaboration, mutual learning, experience sharing, openness, and reflection.

In the responsive circles framework, understanding the various types of circles and the tools available for facilitating them is helpful for creating an environment that fosters healing, accountability, and growth. Circles can serve a range of purposes, from community building to addressing conflict, and the format you choose plays a significant role in achieving your goals. The tools you use to facilitate these circles depends on the structure you choose and the goals of the circle. This chapter will explore different circle types and structures—such as sequential, nonsequential, and digital circles—and the tools that enhance their effectiveness, including talking pieces, documentation tools, timers, lighting, sound machines or music, storyboarding and comic strips, dolls or figures, and the reflection journal. We will also explore circle language, including criminal terminology and affective communication. What's more, I include anecdotes throughout to help paint a clearer picture.

By tailoring circle types and tools to the needs of your students and the unique conflict situations in your settings, you can create safe spaces for meaningful dialogue, reflection, relationship building, and resolution, ensuring every participant feels valued and heard.

Circle Types and Structures

Most commonly, circles come into two types, proactive and reactive, and two structures, sequential and nonsequential. Within the types are subtypes that work depending on the need or the situation. On the other hand, reactive circles are used to address specific incidents of conflict or harm that have occurred within the classroom or school community. These types of circles are held in reaction or in response to something that has happened. Depending on the circle's goal or purpose, facilitators may use a sequential or nonsequential circle structure.

- **Proactive circles** are those that occur on a regular basis. Morning meetings, centering or mindfulness circles, and learning circles are usually facilitated regularly and often have the same goal: to build a strong sense of community, to develop positive connections among members, to establish trust, and to set expectations for the day or an upcoming activity (Costello et al., 2019; Evans & Vaandering, 2016). Educators schedule these circles into their day or put them in their lesson plans. As an example, many educators schedule a morning meeting circle as the way to begin the day with their students. In morning meeting circles, educators often start with a greeting, move into a prompt that asks participants to share something (like what they did over the weekend), and conclude with a look ahead for the week. These are proactive because they're not facilitated in response to anything.

- **Reactive circles** are in response to conflict or harm between students, and their purpose is to repair the harm, resolve the conflict, and reintegrate the person who caused harm back into the classroom or school community. Reactive circles help participants process a problem that already exists and develop a plan for moving forward productively (The Responsive Counselor, n.d.). Responsive circles are one type of reactive circle, and can be either sequential or nonsequential. The steps and purpose are different from proactive meetings, although building and maintaining relationships is at the base of both types.

It is important to understand how you can structure circles. Typically, they follow either a *sequential* format, where participants speak in a specific order, or a *nonsequential* format, where individuals contribute as they feel ready, allowing for conversation to emerge organically. Figure 4.1 shows the overlap among the types.

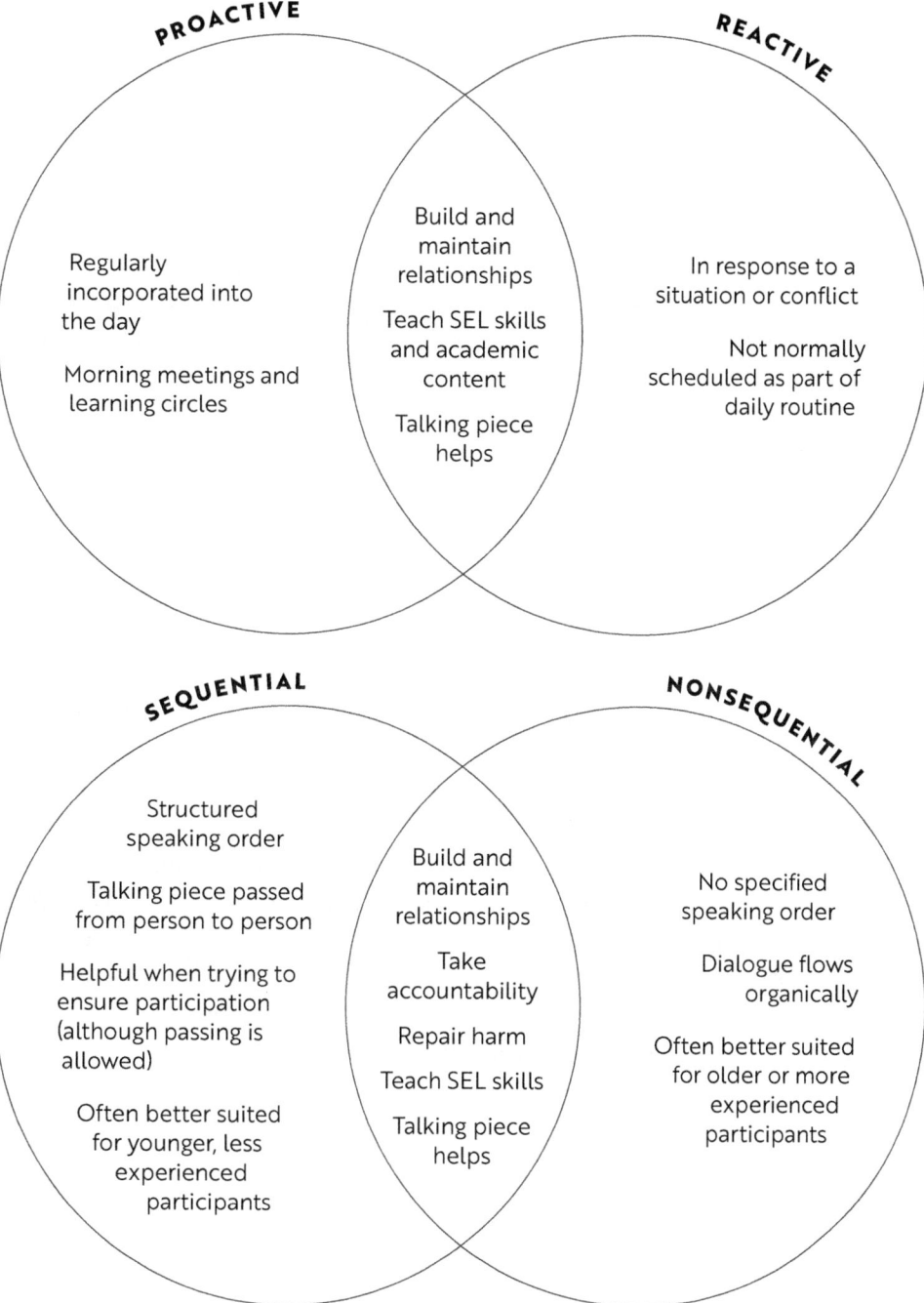

Figure 4.1: Overlaps between circle types.

Sequential Circles

In sequential circles, one person speaks at a time. The chance to speak moves clockwise or counterclockwise around the circle. Sequential structures are often used because they encourage everyone to participate and contribute. In circles, quiet and reserved voices can be silenced by the more assertive voices. With a sequential structure, everyone has an opportunity to speak. In a sequential structure, using agendas, guiding questions, and a talking piece allows participants to express their ideas and share their concerns in a more structured way. There is no back-and-forth discussion in sequential circles. Participants learn to listen more and talk less.

Table 4.1 breaks down the two different types and helps facilitators determine which might work better for their students.

Table 4.1: *Circle Structures That Help Organize the Responsive Circle Process*

SEQUENTIAL	NONSEQUENTIAL
One person speaks at a time	No structured speaking order
Clockwise or counterclockwise progression	Conversation emerges organically
Encourages participation	Participants only share when they have something to say

Source: Adapted from Costello et al., 2019.

Nonsequential Circles

In nonsequential circles, which are more freely structured than sequential circles, conversation emerges and flows organically. The conversation freely travels from one participant to another without established order or direction. Participants only share when they have something to say. This kind of circle requires clear ground rules and expectations. At the onset of every nonsequential circle I facilitate, I clarify the ground rules for speaking and sharing.

In my experience, it's been rare for students to violate speaking or sharing ground rules for nonsequential circles if they're clearly established at the commencement of the circle. If a student does violate a speaking expectation or begins to interrupt other participants, I recommend simply redirecting and reviewing the ground rules or norms. This usually helps get everyone back on track. If this doesn't happen, for some reason, the facilitator can always end the circle and reconvene once all participants are ready to respectfully participate.

Digital Circle Facilitation

Facilitating digital circles is new to most of us. And, to be clear, it is preferable to facilitate circles in person.

The following tips can serve as a strong starting point for facilitating digital circles.

- **Coordinate schedules:** During online learning, I couldn't simply pull students from class to facilitate a circle. Before pulling students from class for circles, I always speak with teachers. When facilitating digital circles, I had to coordinate with more than just the students' teachers. In addition to classroom teachers, I often coordinated schedules with parents. This way, parents could help ensure students were online in time for the circle.

- **Plan and communicate ahead:** During face-to-face circles, I'm comfortable with the conversation evolving organically. With digital circles, however, I found more structure is beneficial. While facilitating digital circles, I started using an agenda. Agendas helped us stay focused, which can be difficult in a virtual setting. I shared this agenda with participants before the actual circle. I would also share the meeting link with participants through email or one of the communication platforms we used (Remind, ClassDojo, and the like). Sometimes, depending on the situation, I would share the meeting link with families, too.

- **Set expectations:** Many educators have passionate feelings about students having their cameras on when learning from home. Some say it helps ensure engagement and participation. Some say students shouldn't be expected to put their cameras on if they don't feel comfortable with the way their home or their room looks. Regardless, in my opinion, students having their cameras on helps establish a more serious tone. I feel that resolving conflict is hard enough in a virtual setting, and becomes even more difficult when students don't have their cameras on. What's more, to minimize distractions, it helps to have participants mute themselves if they're not talking. Finally, if I were facilitating a circle with only two students, it would feel weird if someone were talking and the other participants had their cameras off.

- **Consider privacy:** Now, this is where facilitating digital circles can be tricky. When students were learning virtually, there were times when a parent or guardian would sit next to or near them to provide technological or academic support. Obviously, this is not advised while facilitating a circle with children who are resolving a conflict. Parents are important, and they should be communicated with throughout the process. However, to ensure participants feel safe to participate, it is important only circle participants are present in the virtual meeting. I always assure parents that I will follow up with them at the culmination of the circle.

- **Determine a speaking order:** As I mentioned, while facilitating circles in person, I usually let conversations evolve organically. When I facilitate digital circles, however, I determine a speaking order. This helps prevent distractions and audible issues.

- **Use the chat feature:** I find the chat feature extremely helpful when facilitating a digital circle. In the chat box, I always include the agenda, the speaking order, and a list of questions to consider.

- **Use the talking piece:** I found that talking pieces are helpful when facilitating digital circles. I ask that participants find an object that's meaningful to them and hold it on screen while speaking. This helps show participants who's sharing and who should be listening.

The process steps are otherwise the same.

Circle Facilitation Tools

With effective responsive circles, tools play a critical role in creating a supportive and focused environment. For example, the talking piece ensures each participant has an opportunity to speak, while documentation tools help keep track of important points and agreements. Timers, lighting, and sound can help set a calm, structured environment that promotes psychological safety (Kellenberger, 2022). Additionally, creative tools like storyboarding and comic strips, dolls or figures, and reflection journals offer participants ways to express their thoughts and feelings, especially for younger students or those who find verbal communication challenging. These tools often help facilitate meaningful conversations and reinforce the restorative process.

You won't necessarily use all of the tools listed here, especially not simultaneously, but the options are explained in the following sections.

- Talking piece
- Documentation tool
- Timers
- Lighting and room ambience
- Sound machines or calming music
- Storyboarding and comic strips
- Dolls or figures
- Reflection journal

Read on to learn more about the role each of these tools plays in responsive circles.

Talking Piece

Students in circles may be tempted to talk to each other or over each other, making it necessary to have a tool that ensures everyone knows whose turn it is to speak. A talking piece establishes the rule that whoever has the piece is the only one in the circle doing the talking at that time. Members of the First Nations and other Indigenous groups used various objects as talking pieces for the same purpose; some used a feather, a stick, a sacred shell, or a peace pipe during their circles (First Nations Pedagogy Online, n.d.). In modern responsive circles, the only exception to the talking piece rule is if the facilitator needs to address participant members or clarify something.

In a sequential circle, after the facilitator introduces the circle's purpose, discusses norms, and gives any other directions, the facilitator passes the talking piece to another person. When it comes to which student speaks first, it varies. Most of the time, the facilitator may pose a question from the analyze the harm step (page 47), and a student will chime in with an answer. Other times, facilitators may offer the talking piece to whomever would like to speak first. If students are apprehensive about beginning, the facilitator will speak first and then be patient. Eventually, students will open up. They just need time. On the other hand, in nonsequential circles, the facilitator chooses how the talking piece works. For example, when the facilitator finishes speaking, they may place the talking piece in the center of the circle. Whoever follows takes the piece from the center of the circle, says what they want, and puts it back.

You can use a variety of objects, including a ball, a stuffed animal, a photograph or other image, a rock, or a feather. I've also seen facilitators grab something readily available in the classroom and use it as a talking piece. When selecting a talking piece, it's important to consider the physical needs of all circle participants. For this reason, it's always best to choose an object that's soft, comfortable to hold, and easy to pass. Overall, the talking piece should be inclusive, ensuring it accommodates the comfort and abilities of everyone in circle. Table 4.2 lists pros and cons of some common talking pieces.

Table 4.2: Circle Talking Pieces

PIECE	PROS	CONS
Feather	Soft, safe, and easy to pass	So soft it may get damaged
Stuffed animal	Soft, safe, and easy to pass	Students may be tempted to throw it; gets dirty easily and is difficult to clean
Microphone	Good visual reminder of who should be talking and when	Not very easy to pass
Beach ball	Soft and fairly safe to toss	Can knock over items
Photograph	Depending on the image, can serve as a nice visual reminder of something	Wear and tear happens over time

Regardless of the item a facilitator chooses as the talking piece, it must be safe to pass around. I have found that while circling with students in grades K–3, talking pieces are especially useful for maintaining attention and focus. The pieces can also help inexperienced participants, as they reinforce the norm that we are listening intently while others are talking. Like many aspects of the responsive circle process, the facilitator has the autonomy to decide whether to use and what will serve as a talking piece.

Documentation Tool

It's important to keep notes on the circles for a variety of reasons. For instance, new information may emerge during the circle that did not during the initial investigation. What's more, a physical record gives facilitators something to refer to should future issues occur or if teachers or families have questions about what transpired during the circle. The reproducible "Responsive Circle Notes" (page 66) supports note-taking during circles, and you can visit **go.SolutionTree.com/behavior** for a free online version.

Typically, the notes include categories that align with the steps.

1. **Analyze the harm:** The facilitator simply records what transpired during the incident or the conflict. This will probably read very similarly to investigation notes.
2. **Repair the harm:** The facilitator records how participants plan to make reparations. The facilitator may choose to note whether the suggestions for repairing harm were generated by the students themselves or by the facilitator.
3. **Prevent future harm:** The facilitator records suggestions from participants for preventing the same situation from occurring again.
4. **Make collective commitments:** The facilitator notes the commitments that participants made.
5. **Reintegrate:** The facilitator notes how participants will be reintegrating and what the reintegration progress will entail after checking in with students and staff.

Note-taking works best when the facilitator does it for multiple reasons: if a participant is taking notes, it diminishes their ability to focus. From an efficiency standpoint, most adults can record notes faster than a student. It may be more challenging for student participants to remove biases and only include the facts.

However, in contexts with older students, some facilitators assign a participant the note-taker role. If a participant is assigned the role, it's essential to make your expectations clear before the circle begins. Here are some example expectations.

- **Be confidential:** You must understand the importance of confidentiality and ensure that the notes are shared only with the facilitator and participants.
- **Be focused:** Everyone else will be participating in the conversation. No one will have an opportunity to redirect you, so you must keep yourself focused on your job.
- **Be factual:** Notes include only facts. Do not include feelings or opinions about the conversation or the participants. Your role is to capture what is said, not to offer judgment or commentary.
- **Be discreet:** Take notes quietly and unobtrusively, without disrupting the flow of conversation.
- **Be organized:** Use a note catcher or structured format. You should follow a structured template. This keeps the notes organized and easy to reference later.

It's important that any circle documentation is done in written format because of potential legal or school policy ramifications. Once, while talking to a school dean about facilitating a circle on vaping, he said he wanted to record audio of the circle in case more details emerged. I immediately paused the conversation and warned that he could not do this. Not only would using an audio recording device possibly violate the students' legal rights or a school board policy, but it would also drastically damage the trusting environment necessary to facilitate a successful circle. Details may emerge during a circle. Write them down on paper, but *do not record them* in video or audio.

Timers

Some facilitators find visual timers helpful, especially with lower elementary or inexperienced participants. You can, for example, project a timer on a whiteboard, put a digital timer in the middle of a circle, or use a phone or smartwatch.

Using a timer can change the dynamic of a circle. The presence of timers may make participants feel rushed. They may impact the information shared and the flow of the conversation. If I use a timer, I only do so in a learning circle. I do not use timers while facilitating responsive circles, regardless of the participants' ages or experience levels.

That being said, it's important to be flexible when it comes to time. Allow ample time, but know when to move things along. The time allotments in table 4.3 can be helpful.

Table 4.3: *Common Duration and Participant Totals*

ELEMENTARY	MIDDLE	HIGH
Duration: Fifteen to thirty minutes	**Duration:** Thirty to forty-five minutes	**Duration:** Forty-five minutes to one hour
Participants: Two or three	**Participants:** Between three and five	**Participants:** Between three and seven
Rationale: Younger students have shorter attention spans that usually last between five and fifteen minutes (Mabale, 2023). If circles become too long, students may become restless and unfocused. Shorter circles help them stay engaged and focused. What's more, elementary-level students are typically likely to share information about themselves and their issues.	**Rationale:** Middle school students have an attention span of approximately thirty minutes or less and can often handle longer discussions (Mabale, 2023). If circles get too long or intense, students may need a break. Also, middle school students may be more apprehensive about sharing.	**Rationale:** Usually, high school students are able to engage in deeper, more extended conversations that can last one hour or more. Longer circles can be useful for discussing complex issues or conflicts.

As mentioned, facilitators must be flexible with their time during circles. Some circles at the elementary level may last longer than fifteen or thirty minutes, and some circles at the high school level may not last the full forty-five minutes. It all depends on the severity of the conflict being addressed.

Lighting

Lighting can make a difference in concentration, energy, behavior, and mood (Milosavljevic, 2019; Morrow & Kanakri, 2018). For example, one study on classroom lighting found that students, and especially students with developmental disabilities, were more engaged in classrooms lit with LED lighting (Pulay & Williamson, 2019). A warm or low setting, for instance, can help establish a relaxed atmosphere conducive to sharing and circle dialogue. Students who are dysregulated may benefit from more relaxed atmospheres, especially during circle time when it is supposed to be calm.

Some educators facilitate circles with no lights on. I observed a junior high teacher facilitating a learning circle who turned off all the lights in her room except an old Tiffany-style desk lamp. In other cases, facilitators can turn off the lights but open the shades to allow as much natural light as possible. As always, adapt to meet the needs of students in a variety of activities, including responsive circles (Mogas & Palau, 2021).

Sound Machines or Calming Music

In addition to lighting, some facilitators use white noise or rain sound machines to set a certain vibe. At low settings, these sounds help establish a calming atmosphere. Calming music or nature sounds, including chirping birds, rustling leaves, or the sound of crashing waves, can lower cortisol levels, reduce anxiety and stress, and promote relaxation (Audiophil.io, 2023; Groarke, Groarke, Hogan, Costello, & Lynch, 2020; Groarke & Hogan, 2019). I once observed a teacher facilitate a circle with quiet orchestral music playing. While debriefing with the teacher, she said the music lightened the mood and created a comfortable environment for her students. She clarified, however, that if she were facilitating a more serious circle, she would not use music at all.

Storyboarding and Comic Strips

Storyboarding graphic organizers and comic strips can be helpful communication tools for students, especially if a participant has difficulty communicating verbally. What's more, drawing—including using comic strips—can help students express complex ideas and vocabulary, convey narratives, and share their emotions (Reach & Teach, n.d.; Sarada, 2016; Wijaya, Suwastini, Adnyani, & Adnyani, 2021).

I've never used comic strips, but I have facilitated a circle where students drew their story. A student, Maria, and her parents had immigrated to the United States with a caravan of other families from the same small town in Venezuela. She spoke no English. One day, Maria bit a classmate while waiting in the lunch line. Fortunately, the student Maria bit was wearing a fleece jacket. There was no broken skin and barely a mark. Regardless, after a trip to the nurse's office, my initial investigation, and the family phone calls, I facilitated a circle with the students involved. I knew this would be challenging, not only because of their ages (they were seven) but also because of a potential language barrier. A bilingual staff member and I communicated to the two students how the circle would work. During the circle, Maria drew what happened in the incident. It turned out that the other student stuck her tongue out at Maria. The other student had not revealed this at first. (Note that I did not conduct a full investigation before the circle, as the bilingual staff member was unavailable and had limited time to assist with translation. If I had conducted a full investigation with the help of the bilingual translator, this would have surfaced prior to the circle.) It didn't excuse the biting, but the drawing did inform everyone further. Since then, I've incorporated visuals into various circles when there may be communication challenges or when students are apprehensive to verbally discuss the incident. Sometimes, drawing helps reluctant students share more information about certain situations.

Using visuals such as storyboarding and comic strips can help students express themselves. This is especially important and relevant for English learners or students with communication challenges. That said, this may be a new approach to learning or expression for some students, so it would behoove educators to have patience with themselves and their students as they use this strategy.

Dolls or Figures

Using dolls or figures as a tool in responsive circles can help students communicate more openly, participate in group discussions, and develop empathy skills (Hashmi, Vanderwert, Paine, & Gerson, 2021; Papouli, 2019). This can be especially helpful for early elementary students, as well as those with communication challenges, who might be apprehensive about participating or are new to a language. Dolls and figures offer a physical, non-threatening medium through which young people can communicate and project their emotions or ideas. By interacting with dolls or figures, students can externalize their thoughts in a creative and engaging way.

Also, this approach can be very helpful when resolving a student conflict that involves some type of physical altercation. It's particularly helpful when that altercation involves K–2 students. For example, during a circle I facilitated with primary students, one moving along very efficiently, the co-facilitating social worker handed one of the students a doll and asked her to point on the doll where the other student had physically contacted her. It turned out that one of the girls bumped the other while waiting in line. Though you have to be on the lookout to ensure something like a doll or figure isn't a distraction, they could help in situations like the one described here.

Reflection Journal

Using a reflection journal after participating in a responsive circle can benefit students. Writing in a journal helps students process their thoughts and emotions, encourages deeper self-reflection, can prompt metacognition, and assists students in understanding their own perspectives as well as the feelings and viewpoints of others (Alt, Raichel, & Naamati-Schneider, 2022; Chen & Forbes, 2014; Dinç, Wherley, & Sankey, 2024). Better-developed empathy and self-reflection skills from reflective journaling could lead to better decision making and the prevention of the same or similar conflicts in the future. What's more, it can provide an outlet for students who have found it difficult to fully express themselves during the circle, offering them the opportunity to articulate their experiences and insights at their own pace.

I provide students with these reflection journals if they decide they'd like to reflect more on the circle. You can provide participants with hard copies of the reproducible "Responsive Circle Reflection" (page 70). They can write about anything they may be thinking about, including the following as an example.

- How they thought the circle transpired
- If there's something they'd change about the process
- How they feel now
- Any progress they've made toward keeping their collective commitments
- Any challenges they've had keeping their collective commitments
- If any issues have persisted after the circle

Reflection journals also help with the check-in process. Students may like to reference their reflections and share some of the things they've been thinking about since the circle concluded. Page 54 explains collective commitments, and page 58 explains post-circle debriefs and check-ins.

Most of the time, unless sharing updates with the facilitator during check-in, students keep their journals private. However, I once facilitated a circle with two students who'd participated in a circle together for a different conflict. For this new conflict and circle, both students brought their reflection journals with them to reference how they had been making progress since the previous circle. It was eye-opening that sharing from reflection journals could be helpful, especially for repeated conflicts and participants. That said, sharing is voluntary, as things written in reflection journals can be very personal.

Circle Language

In responsive circles, language plays a critical role in shaping the experience and outcomes. Criminal terminology, such as labeling behaviors or individuals *offenders*, *criminals*, *delinquent*, or *victims*, can reinforce negative identities and perpetuate a punitive mindset, since "labeled individuals may eventually come to view themselves as criminals and act in accord with this self-concept" (Marshall, 2024). This language, which students often internalize, labels individuals according to their mistakes rather than their potential for growth and change.

In contrast, affective language emphasizes emotions and personal experiences, helping participants express how they feel and how they have been affected by others' actions. By shifting from criminal terminology to affective language, responsive circles foster a more compassionate and constructive dialogue, focused on healing, reparation, and accountability.

Avoid Criminal Terminology

It's important for facilitators to be mindful of the terminology participants use during circle. Just as it is advisable to avoid labeling students based on their academic performances, it is a good idea to avoid labeling them for their actions, because the terminology tends to label the students instead of the behaviors.

Criminalizing terminology—*offender*, *perpetrator*, and *victim*, for example—stigmatizes students and leads to them perceiving themselves as deviants (Bramley, Hall, Ely, & Robin-D'Cruz, n.d.). In other words, "Labels which focus on experiences of violence [or conflict, in this case], presuppose an individual's inability to change or undergo personal development, to transform their identity into a peaceful, empowered personality" (Partners for Prevention, n.d., p. 3).

In my experience, it felt wrong (and bizarre) to call a six-year-old an *offender*. Elementary students don't even know what those words mean, and such labels damage student dignity, hurt the trusting relationships you are trying to build, shape students' self-perceptions, and are antithetical to an environment focused on repair and forgiveness (Denver, Ballou, & DeWitt, 2024; Kayama, Haight, Gibson, & Wilson, 2015).

Phrases such as *those who've been harmed* and *those who have caused harm* are pretty cumbersome. (Consider, for example, "John, who harmed Alex by stealing money out of his locker" or "JR, who was harmed by Alex when he called him a name.") Consider simply using student names while facilitating circles. The majority of the time, students know why they're in a circle and how they've been harmed. They don't need a label like *offender* to clarify that.

Use language that is developmentally appropriate for your students, maintains student dignity, develops trusting relationships, and helps facilitate repair and forgiveness. Use language that separates the offender from the offense, the doer from the deed, as given here (Ortega, Lyubansky, Nettles, & Espelage, 2016).

- Instead of *harmer* or *offender*: *Author*
- Instead of *person harmed* or *victim*: *Receiver*

As a middle school co-principal, I facilitated a circle between two students—one had her hat stolen, and the other student was the person implicated in taking it. This circle occurred before I changed my terminology, so I referred to the person who the investigation revealed had stolen the hat as *offender*. Overall, the process went extremely well. The student returned the hat, made other reparations, and the two became friendly. When debriefing the teachers on the success of the circle, I continued using criminal terminology while referring to the students. I described how the "offender" stole the "victim's" hat. Fast forward a few weeks later to a different incident that occurred between some girls. After the resulting circle, I followed up with the same team for debrief. One of the teachers asked if the original student was involved, since she was the "offender" in the hat theft. The label transcended different conflicts. I set the wrong example.

Use Affective Communication

If the goal is to move away from criminal terminology, the question becomes what to replace it with. As noted in the previous section, no specific labels are necessary in most cases. However, there are contexts for which a shared language is helpful. I find that using language that better incorporates empathy or encourages empathy is extremely beneficial for circle outcomes.

As one of the most important life skills, empathy is the backbone of responsive circles and what makes the process so effective at resolving and preventing future conflict. When students have the opportunity to practice empathy in restorative settings, they are more likely to develop prosocial behaviors, foster deeper connections with others, think about and understand the feelings and experiences of others, and engage constructively in the circle process. This leads to a more supportive and inclusive school environment (Lown, 2016; Nelson-Simley, 2020; Wallis, 2014). In fact, when describing the difference between restorative practices or responsive circles compared to more traditional discipline or conflict management approaches, empathy is the element that makes the difference.

Two second-grade students who had an intense argument during recess were in circle with me. Jamie wouldn't let Alex play soccer with a group of their peers. Alex explained how hurt he felt after being excluded, since he thought they were friends. It was quiet for a minute. I encouraged Jamie to take a deep breath and listen to Alex's words again, this time focusing on how Alex might feel. After hearing Alex verbalize his feelings a second time, Jamie said that he didn't realize how much he had hurt Alex and hadn't considered how leaving him out would impact him. The tension immediately started to ease. This helped them both see the situation from each other's perspectives. By acknowledging the hurt, Jamie took responsibility for his actions, and Alex felt heard and validated. Jamie made a commitment to include Alex in future games and to speak up if he saw others being excluded.

As important as empathy is, it can be challenging to teach and difficult to learn. Researchers indicate the following types of empathy (Hodges & Myers, 2007).

- **Emotional:** Having the same feelings as someone else
- **Cognitive:** How well someone can correctly identify another person's thoughts and feelings and whether we understand we have successfully done that

As such, circles are the perfect opportunity for both facilitators to teach empathy and for students to learn and experience empathy.

Effective facilitators employ empathetic communication throughout all stages of the circle. The best form of communication that helps emphasize empathy in responsive circles is referred to as affective communication. *Affective communication* is the exchange of feelings, emotions, and attitudes between individuals (Costello et al., 2019).

Table 4.4 compares typical versus affective communication examples. It involves both verbal and nonverbal cues that demonstrate emotions and help to establish rapport, understanding, and empathy. Affective communication is essential for building strong

Table 4.4: Typical Versus Affective Communication

TYPICAL COMMUNICATION	AFFECTIVE COMMUNICATION
"Stealing the iPad was bad."	"When you stole my iPad, it made me feel sad and unsafe."
"Calling people names is not nice."	"When you called me stupid, it made me feel angry and upset."
"Defacing school property is against the rules."	"When you defaced school property, it disappointed the custodian and made more work for him."

relationships and interpersonal connections. It requires that an individual use *feeling language* when sharing how something, usually another person's actions, has impacted them.

To use affective communication, share a small, developmentally appropriate bit of yourself and your feelings during circles. For example, I once facilitated a circle with two students, one of whom said he was experiencing stress and anxiety. He explained that he was mean to his classmate because he was feeling anxious and couldn't control his anger. After saying that, he started to cry. The other student went to respond, and I raised my hand to signal that we needed a minute. I could tell he was being truthful about his anxiety. He was struggling. I shared with the circle that I'm also an anxious person and that I, too, have trouble controlling my emotions when I'm super anxious. I used an example of yelling at one of my children for something small when I was feeling that way. Both students looked at me in shock. It's easy to forget that our students might look at us as if we're without flaws, especially those similar to their own. The dynamic in the circle changed. Participation increased. Disclosing personal information in this way, especially regarding how something made us feel or how something impacted us, is a way of using affective communication with circle participants. It also helps build trust and creates stronger connections among circle participants (Altenmüller, Kampschulte, Verbeek, & Gollwitzer, 2023; Liu, Min, Zhai, & Smyth, 2016).

Importantly, this sharing depends on how comfortable the facilitator is with self-disclosure. I recall Mrs. Baker, one of my seventh-grade teachers, facilitating a circle with two students who had stolen her district-issued iPad. After I conducted the initial investigation, both students agreed to participate in a responsive circle with Mrs. Baker as the facilitator. I wasn't sure about this dynamic, where Mrs. Baker, the person who was harmed in this situation, would actually facilitate the circle. I offered to do it. But, Mrs. Baker insisted. Right from the start, the students were very unresponsive and indifferent. In fact, during introductions, they stared at the floor without lifting their heads.

Eventually, after about five minutes of silence, I almost recommended Mrs. Baker end the circle and reconvene at a later time. This was until she started disclosing how the students stealing the iPad actually made her feel. She shared how it made her sad, disappointed, frustrated, and scared. She explained how she used the iPad in small groups with her students and how they liked using apps on the device. She also described how she worked long and hard planning many of the lessons stored on that iPad. She talked about how she always wanted to make sure her students had interesting and engaging lessons and how all that planning actually took time away from the time she could have been spending with her daughter at home. Finally, she mentioned how devastated her daughter would be to learn that the iPad was stolen, as she often used it at home.

It was at this moment that the dynamic changed. The students raised their heads from the floor, glanced over at each other, and then at their teacher. One of the students apologized right then and there. The other immediately followed. Mrs. Baker wasn't really even talking about reparations or how the students could make the situation right (yet). She was just opening up about how the theft made her feel. To her credit, her self-disclosure did the trick. After she explained how the theft made her and her daughter feel, the students were thoroughly engaged and seemed intent on making things right. This is as clear and stark an example as you're likely to find of how important empathy is to the entire conflict resolution process.

Many students are experts at making us think they don't care or that they're too cool to care. Before these two boys heard about the impact their actions had on their teacher and her daughter, they were completely apathetic. When the boys were made to feel how their teacher felt or how her daughter felt, their attitudes completely changed. The teacher delivered these statements in such a way that the boys felt her sadness. They felt how disappointed she was. They felt how sad their teacher's daughter would be. They were disappointed in themselves for making their teacher and her daughter feel sad.

Either with your team or on your own, respond to the discussion questions and consider what next steps to take with the following guidance.

DISCUSSION QUESTIONS

How do you embed empathy in your current practice? Academically? Behaviorally?

How would you embed more affective communication in responsive circles? In curriculum content? In conversations with team members? In conversations with parents?

Suppose you're facilitating a circle at the secondary school level. The conflict occurred outside school and involved harassment over social media channels. Unfortunately, the conflict, though it occurred outside school, is negatively impacting the learning environment. What circle structure would you use? What tools would you use? How would you use affective communication in this circle?

NEXT STEPS

Create your own talking piece. As a team, create a meaningful talking piece together. Ask each person to contribute ideas or materials for a talking piece that represents shared values. This engages team members creatively and strengthens investment in the process.

Design circle prompts for different situations. With your team, develop a set of circle prompts or questions tailored to different scenarios. Having a toolbox of prompts prepared in advance can help facilitators feel more confident and flexible when facilitating circles in various contexts and for various reasons.

Reflect using your personal reflection journal. It's helpful when students use a reflection journal after circles. It's helpful for facilitators, too. Begin journaling after each circle to reflect on what went well and what could be improved, even if it's a practice circle.

CHAPTER 5

Resistance and Resource Constraints

"Dr. E, you have a call on line one. It's Miguel Gamez's mom," my secretary informed me.

I greeted her after we were connected, and Mrs. Gamez asked, "What's this circle thing you did with Miguel yesterday?" I had explained it on the phone with her prior to the circle, per my preparation steps, but she needed a debrief, so I took that opportunity to reexplain.

"Miguel instigated a conflict with another student. The responsive circle between him and the other student was an effort to productively resolve the conflict and prevent future issues."

"When you said 'circle' on the phone yesterday, I thought it would be some kind of punishment—not a therapy session." I thanked her for her feedback at the end of the call.

A week later, Miguel was in my office for saying hurtful things to another student. After completing another responsive circle, I called both families to discuss it.

The next morning, Mrs. Gamez was on the phone with me. She explained that Miguel had been quiet when he got home from school, which is not like him. When she checked on him, he was writing something.

"I'm happy to hear he was getting started on his homework right away," I replied.

"It wasn't his homework. He was writing an apology letter to a girl in school." Mrs. Gamez revealed that she was initially opposed to circles, but this was the first time she'd seen Miguel consider his own behavior and how he hurt someone else's feelings.

She explained, "I think he got to see things through someone else's eyes."

Change is difficult. It always will be. Even the best, most well-intentioned change is a challenge. As educators, we can plan and plan and plan some more when it comes to a change or new initiative. We can communicate the plan until we're blue in the face. We can provide visual diagrams and detailed change plans that clearly explain every step along the way. We can clearly explain how people will receive ongoing support as they embrace the change. We can inform parents and community members up front and often.

That said, change requires an adjustment to daily procedures and routines. Change requires that we do things differently. For many, change is also a mindset shift that requires us to step outside our comfort zones and think differently. For Miguel's mom, this "new way of disciplining students" required a mindset shift on her part as the parent, a shift that took her time to become comfortable with.

Regardless of how well leaders plan, communicate, and provide support, change is almost always accompanied by uncertainty, increased levels of stress and anxiety, and the fear of the unknown. What makes change even more challenging is one-and-done initiatives that never last. The predictable questions like "What's it gonna be this year?" or "How long will this last?" come to mind. Further, there are resource constraints involved in the implementation of change, even with something as relatively straightforward as responsive circles. So, yes, change is hard. It takes time. It requires effort and commitment. But that doesn't mean we stop striving for improvement and growth. That doesn't mean we're pleased with the status quo. Fortunately, there are steps we leaders can take to ease the acceptance of change, and you'll learn about these steps in this chapter.

Implementation Resistance

Leading the charge for the implementation of responsive circles involves getting buy-in from a lot of different stakeholders. The example that leads this chapter highlights just one form of skepticism about circle efficacy that you might encounter from a student's family. Other forms of resistance might come from teachers, support staff, or even members of your school's leadership team. This means you need to get ahead of that resistance by building a compelling case for responsive circles that addresses the priorities of these different stakeholder groups. What's more, forming a supportive coalition to support this change is helpful. With your team, advocating for this change to all stakeholders is important (Marzano, Waters, & McNulty, 2005).

Before planning a new initiative or major change, such as implementing responsive circles, consult a variety of information sources. For instance, the building leadership team may have reasons for a new initiative. Maybe schoolwide student achievement data or attendance reports suggest improvement is necessary. Or maybe the feedback generated from recent parent surveys reveals a need.

Whatever it is, identify data or information that help paint a picture of what needs to be improved and why. For instance, compile the following data before the end of your current school year.

- State- or province-specific data
- Office disciplinary referrals
- Conflict or bullying incident referrals

- Detention rates
- Suspension rates
- School attendance and tardiness data
- Student and teacher surveys

Identify trending areas of growth and deficiency. See how the deficiency impacts different subgroup populations and grade levels. For example, data from national surveys suggest that boys, students of color, neurodivergent students, and students from low socioeconomic backgrounds are punished using traditional disciplinary measures at much higher rates than their White peers, even for the same offenses (Achilles et al., 2007; Brobbey, 2018; de Brey et al., 2019; Fabelo et al., 2011; Office for Civil Rights, 2016; Zhang et al., 2004). Alternatively, maybe you noticed a major increase in office referrals for physical altercations during recess. If you and your team notice trends like these, it's time to rethink how discipline and conflict are managed in your school. Consider conducting a comparative analysis using the same criteria to see how other schools in the same district or area are doing.

After compiling and analyzing the requisite data, share them with your building leadership team or other educators in the building. Communicate the information in a very clear and concise presentation. Most times, if the trend data are compelling enough, they speak for themselves. If, for some reason, the data aren't compelling, ask the team to find additional data that either refute the identified need or make the case for prioritizing a different need. Come to this meeting prepared to share a few evidence-based strategies for improving the deficiency.

Then, give examples of ways you plan to support staff with the new initiative. After sharing the need, potential initiatives for improvement, and support examples, open the floor for discussion with the team. After discussing and developing a plan, begin meeting with grade-level or teaching teams to share it. I like to begin sharing this information in my weekly staff newsletter and in monthly staff meetings early and often. This way, it's no surprise when it comes time to actually implement the change.

Whatever your approach, the goal is to clearly establish the need for change or a new initiative, identify a few different initiatives that would address the need if implemented, and communicate a staff support plan, all before the end of the current school year. This gives staff time to ponder the information, formulate questions, and consider any other support they may need to make the initiative successful. They can share questions and ideas with you or leadership team members. During the last leadership meeting of the year, the team can consider the current support plan and any support ideas or questions generated by other staff members and address or include them if necessary.

This work pays off by first starting small, ensuring you find your initial group of advocates in the school leadership team and then the building. These advocates will help you promote and educate about the implementation of responsive circles and expand that group steadily outward to eventually include all stakeholders, both inside and outside the building.

It should be noted that regardless of how much we involve stakeholders in the process or how well the new initiative is planned or how much and how clearly we communicate the change, there will always be bumps when rubber meets the road. As you implement responsive circles, you will meet some resistance and resource shortcomings from educators, from families and the community, and from students. The following sections address how to plan for and respond to this resistance.

Educator Resistance

Educators are busy, hardworking people. As such, it can be hard to consider new approaches or different strategies that take time. To some, restorative practices and responsive circles may even seem inefficient. That said, I find there is a mindset shift that helps tremendously when it comes to using responsive circles to help students resolve conflict. Rather than seeing conflict as a problem, as a drag on time, or as something someone else in the building should deal with (like the social worker, if you're a principal), I view conflict as an opportunity to build and strengthen relationships with my students. It's an opportunity to learn more about each other, connect and build community, and mend and repair relationships. It's an opportunity to grow in learning and self-improvement and roll up your sleeves and teach. I find this mindset shift extremely motivating. It gets me involved and devoted to finding the necessary space and time to ensure conflict resolution and support happen in my school. Besides, not only is addressing conflict important for preventing further issues, but it is also all in the name of building better relationships with students.

Remember that when it comes to staff pushback, it helps to predict why staff may resist a certain change or initiative. With restorative practices, teachers and staff may resist adopting new methods or approaches if they're comfortable with existing practices. In addition, staff may resist change if they see new initiatives as being at odds with their own beliefs and philosophies. One staff member described this approach as "too forgiving." When issues like this occur, talk one-to-one with staff members and explain that if we truly want students to learn a lesson, there has to be an opportunity for learning. I further explain that as a circle facilitator, in order to successfully resolve conflicts and repair harm while also maintaining relationships, I capitalize on opportunities to model and teach social-emotional learning competencies like empathy and self-awareness. It takes time to develop this kind of shared meaning and understanding with staff, but it is important for the success of any change or initiative (Fullan, 2007).

In addition to personal conversations, clearly communicate why this is important and include supporting data. In addition to articulating how the change will benefit students, it helps to explain how the change will positively improve the entire school community, such as how it helps build relationships among students and staff, cultivate positive school culture and climate, diminish traditional power imbalances and structures, and reduce recidivism (Costello et al., 2019; Diliberti & Schwartz, 2023; EAB, 2023; Mills et al., 2019; Strang et al., 2013; Wang, 2023). Leaders who can effectively make the case that a change will also benefit the adults in the building have a better chance of mitigating resistance.

Furthermore, change is hard on a leader or the change agent, too. No one person has the influence, energy, or expertise to completely facilitate the entire change process all by themselves, regardless of how effective a circle facilitator or leader they are. Building a team dedicated to supporting the work of responsive circles can help when planning, communicating, supporting, and managing the change initiative. Many times, those who support the idea or the change are of equal or more importance than the change itself (Bambrick-Santoyo, 2018; Patterson, Grenny, Maxfield, McMillan, & Switzler, 2008). This team, which is analogous to the concept of a guiding coalition in professional learning communities, is composed of key staff members or early adopters already open to the change (DuFour et al., 2024; Kotter, 2012).

Because embracing and implementing something like restorative practices is a fairly sizable change, especially when it comes to staff mindsets, leading the team through the process of creating a new mission and vision can be helpful. It is also beneficial for the leader of this team to recruit parents or other community members as they develop the new mission and vision. In my experience, we focused on clearly communicating how our utilization of restorative practices and circles would result in healthy reparations of harm, the prevention of future harm, the maintenance and cultivation of relationships, and the successful resolution of conflict. Parental involvement in this process helps spread the message throughout the community, too. Given this, let's look at some ways to address pushback from this stakeholder group.

Family and Community Resistance

Staff pushback won't be the only adult resistance. Leaders will also face resistance from families or other adult community members. Similar to staff resistance, families often resist because responsive practices and circles may be at odds with their own personal beliefs. Everyone (or at least mostly everyone) has gone to school, and they all have opinions about how schools should operate.

Most people base those opinions on personal experiences. As the saying goes, "experience is the best teacher" (Dwyer, 2021). However, those personal experiences aren't always generalizable to the population at large. What's more, educators should be reasonably certain that parents have probably heard about restorative practices or restorative justice online. Misinformation is common and requires correcting by sharing data and evidence-based research. Communications and meetings are two methods for disseminating information that help cultivate family and community buy-in.

Communications

When I was hired as the principal in a well-established and fairly traditional school district, I remember a parent called my office to discuss the parent letter I sent home to introduce families to the concept of responsive circles. He had a lot of questions about circles as I described them in my letter. He talked about research he'd done on restorative practices and how he'd read that they're actually a system for indoctrination. I articulated my views on restorative practices, especially as they pertain to relationships, reparation, forgiveness, closure, and conflict resolution. As our conversation was ending, he asked, "So, do you guys not give suspensions anymore, then?" Based on that conversation, I knew a letter to families would not be enough.

While an initial letter alone will not get buy-in from all families, it is a place to start the communication process. In my experience, such communication must come early and often. At the beginning of the year, start by sending a letter home with students like the one shown in figure 5.1.

Dear families,

As you may know, we take relationships very seriously at our school. We work extremely hard to cultivate a safe, welcoming, nurturing, and trusting environment for our students. We believe students thrive in a school that emphasizes relationships as the foundation for all learning.

Nevertheless, in school, things happen. Students have disagreements. Occasionally, these disagreements may lead students to make poor decisions or react impulsively and without thinking. Many times, students don't fully understand how these disagreements impact the entire school community. Some disagreements can impact relationships in an entire class, a grade level, or the whole school.

To that end, we see these conflicts as opportunities to foster or deepen relationships. Therefore, we employ a restorative approach when helping students solve their problems and resolve their conflicts. The most common tool in our toolbox is the responsive circle. Responsive circles help repair harm between students and within the entire school community, and they also help students cultivate lifelong skills such as empathy and self-reflection. These skills will help students proactively address conflict throughout their lives.

During the year, your child may be invited to participate in a responsive circle. As mentioned, these circles afford students an opportunity to address and resolve conflicts they may have with their peers. Your child's participation in the circle is voluntary. If they feel uncomfortable participating, they will not be forced to do so. As always, whether I facilitate a circle with your child or not, you will be informed of any disciplinary situations involving your child.

If you have any questions, please do not hesitate to contact me.

Dr. JR Entsminger
Principal

Figure 5.1: *Parent letter for responsive circles.*

I also have hard copies of the letter available at back-to-school night, which is usually the evening before students return to school from summer break. Make sure to have the letter translated in all languages spoken by families attending your school.

Meetings

Meetings with presentations can also provide some clarification. Meeting parents on their own turf can also go a long way, as well. For instance, if you're experiencing heavy resistance from parents, consider hosting a meeting at the local public library or recreation center. For whatever reason, I find that some families don't always feel comfortable coming to school. Hosting the meeting at a local community gathering space might not only increase attendance, but it can also demonstrate commitment to the initiative. This aligns with the idea of overlapping spheres of influence. When the school, family, and community are involved in an initiative, the likelihood of support and success increases (Epstein, Sanders, & Sheldon, 2019).

With the initial information available for families to access, the next step is to ensure they have access to you or other members of the team supporting responsive circles. Inform families and community members that your team is always available to take their questions regarding circles. Make yourself or other members of your team available for them to email or call to get more information.

Suggestions for hosting a meeting are as follows.

- **Create a welcoming environment.**
  - *Build trust*—Inviting families into the school building is great, but some schools have better success with this than others. If attendance at these events is low, consider hosting the meeting at a community staple (library, park, or community center, for example). Begin by welcoming families and acknowledging their role in the school community. Consider using restorative and affective language (page 82) to set the tone for mutual respect and collaboration.
  - *Make the setup inclusive*—Arrange the room in a circle, mirroring the responsive circle setup, to model the practice for parents and foster a sense of equality and community from the start. Consider using a talking piece as well.
- **Set clear goals for the meeting.**
  - *State the objective*—Clearly define the meeting's purpose, such as educating families on what restorative practices and responsive circles are and how they will benefit students.
  - *State the desired outcome*—Make sure families leave with a solid understanding of how these practices build community, improve relationships, and support conflict resolution.
- **Use clear, accessible language.**
  - *Avoid jargon*—Explain restorative practices and responsive circles using plain language. Define terms like *accountability*, *repairing harm*, *recidivism*, and *community building* in ways that relate to home and everyday family life.

- *Provide examples*—Share general stories of how restorative practices have helped students in the school resolve conflicts or feel more included. *Do not* include personally identifiable student information in your examples.
- *Offer translation support*—If you have students or families who speak a language other than English, have translation support.

○ **Demonstrate a circle in action.**
- *Do a live demonstration*—Consider running a short mock responsive circle with a group of teachers or students to demystify the process.
- *Compare responsive circles to punishment*—Highlight the key differences between punishments that most parents are familiar with and the responsive circle stages. (Punishments exclude students from the school community, put students on a path toward future problems, fail to address the underlying behavior issues, and ignore an opportunity to teach life skills. Responsive circles reduce the use of traditional punitive discipline, positively build relationships, cultivate and maintain positive school and workplace culture, reduce power structures, enhance soft skill development—empathy especially—and increase shared accountability.)

○ **Explain the benefits for students and families.**
- *Students and families*—Be clear on the benefits for students, including the stronger relationships, skills like empathy and active listening, and reduced repeated conflict and subsequent disciplinary issues. Be sure to remind families of the benefits to them—a more positive school environment and essential-skills use (and their reinforcement) at home, and increased levels of accountability taking.
- *Staff and school community*—Encourage staff to share stories or examples regarding changes they've seen in students who have participated in responsive circles, such as increased responsibility taking, less student conflict, and fewer disciplinary issues. What's more, it can be helpful to have local businesses or organizations from the community share how skills like empathy and active listening learned during responsive circles are in high demand in the workplace.

○ **Take questions and feedback.**
- *Use technology*—Display a QR code on a large screen or hand out flyers with a QR code families can scan, which takes them to a Google Form collecting feedback.
- *Close the loop*—If someone uses the QR code to ask questions, get back to them. Calling them to address their questions goes a long way in establishing trust with families.

Student Participation

Circles are usually new to students. Thus, they tend to have many questions. Kindergartners and first graders may have questions just because they're new to school and because there are multiple stages in the process.

Though you might communicate extensively about circles with the community, remember that responsive circles may not directly impact all students in the school. Yes, students engage in morning meeting circles or teaching and learning circles or getting-to-know-you circles, but the majority of students don't participate in a responsive circle, especially as they progress to higher levels of secondary education. When setting schoolwide or classroom expectations with students at the beginning of the year, make clear that circles are included as a way to develop and maintain relationships and resolve conflicts. For example, a principal can share circle information during the beginning-of-year assembly. Include them in your "Welcome to my classroom!" letter to families and behavior expectation norm setting with students. Additionally, like with the implementation of most school initiatives, it helps when we involve students in the process. When students feel they have a voice and choice in something, there's often more interest and buy-in (Cavanagh et al., 2016; Gale & Parker, 2014; Zion, 2009).

I worked in a district where the superintendent asked the district principals, in collaboration with classroom teachers, to choose upper-elementary students to participate in his student advisory council. This council would meet a few times a year, and during these meetings, students were able to provide feedback on certain events or initiatives happening in the district. What's more, the students in the council would also ideate with the superintendent on upcoming events, activities, and fundraisers. Naturally, the students involved in this committee felt their voices were being heard, and as a result, they expressed increased interest in school happenings. Building leaders can and should do the same thing. While considering the implementation of circles, leaders can put together a committee of students to help generate ideas and solutions about implementation. When students involved in these committees go home and share the information with their parents or guardians, it helps spread the message throughout the community.

Implementation Resource Constraints

While the benefits of responsive circles in promoting a positive school culture, nurturing social-emotional learning skills like empathy, and fostering productive conflict resolution are clear, schools often face resource constraints that impede implementation. Many times, those resource constraints include time, staffing, funding, training, turnover, and sustainability issues. The following sections address each of those constraints and offer some ideas for working with or around them.

Time

Like all things worth doing, responsive circles take time, requiring relationship building, pre-facilitation and facilitation, post-circle check-ins, healthy relationship maintenance, and prevention. Of course, time is something we'll never have enough of. Prioritizing and exercising some creativity with scheduling can help. For instance, schools and classrooms at elementary and secondary levels can integrate responsive circles into existing classroom time.

- **Elementary level:** Teachers and administrators could work together to incorporate responsive circles into the daily morning meeting portion of the day. Not only would this support social-emotional learning, but it also sets a positive tone for the day. As another example, elementary level educators could use transitions and downtime for responsive circle implementation. Many schools and classrooms have post-recess or post-lunch recharge time. During this time, students get a chance to read, relax, and recharge before reengaging in academic tasks. Scheduling responsive circles during this time can help manage conflicts or social dynamics that arise during these inherently less structured parts of the school day.

- **Middle school and high school levels:** Educators can restructure existing schedules or blocks to incorporate responsive circles. I worked with a team of middle school administrators who incorporated responsive circle time into their homeroom or advisory periods. The periods were redesigned from a study hall focus to a focus on emotional check-ins, conflict resolution, and relationship building activities. These kinds of time investments up front pay off when it comes to decreasing recidivism, minimizing instructional time students miss because of punishments like suspension, and ameliorating other disruptions due to student conflict (Anyon et al., 2016; Kline, 2016; Samimi, Han, Navvab, Sedivy, & Anyon, 2023).

As a building leader, I have found some ways to structure and prioritize my own time that allow me to facilitate circles when necessary. Sometimes, this requires that I set clear boundaries. When my door is closed, and the sign says *Circle in Progress*, I'm busy. Obviously, emergencies happen. If it's an emergency that puts students or staff in harm's way, I have to take care of that. But, most of the time, it's not an emergency. Sometimes, the time investment requires that I lean on other staff members for help. I may ask that the building's social worker handle another behavior-related issue while I'm in a circle. I may ask my secretary to hold all my calls while I'm in a circle. I may need to reschedule a non-essential meeting or two. I may have to facilitate circles only during parts of the day that are less busy. For instance, if I notice that I'm handling or resolving a lot of issues after recess, I may try to schedule circles for the morning if possible. Or, if I notice that I'm doing more teacher observations in the morning than the afternoon, I'll schedule circles for the afternoons. For other educators, such as the social worker or guidance counselor, they may be able to schedule regular circle time into their daily sessions or integrate circles into their regular practice or curriculum.

Clearly, this is easier said than done. Students have busy schedules, too. Students have specials, band, core instructional time, lunch, recess, and more. But, when I set the expectation that circles are a priority for me, I make it happen.

Staffing

Restorative practices and responsive circles need proper staffing to be truly effective. It's hard to make circles work when there's only one itinerant staff member who has the time to manage student conflicts. In some buildings, itinerants like social workers can help facilitate some circles here and there. However, it's important to remember that social workers do have lots of other responsibilities, including caseloads full of students who have legal minutes. Also, we don't want to send the message that any time there's a conflict, it's the social worker's responsibility to resolve it. Thus, for educators working in lean settings, it can be challenging to find the staff necessary to help support circles. I am a building principal and facilitate all responsive circles in my building. The building's social worker may participate. But, as the leader, I do all the pre-circle work, facilitate, and conduct all post-circle work. In a middle school or high school setting, where there's usually a number of assistant principals, deans, counselors, or social workers, facilitating responsive circles may be a bit more realistic. An all-hands-on-deck approach can help with the overall implementation.

Here is an example from one superintendent I know of how to get creative with staffing in support of circle implementation. This person and his team noticed students were accumulating excessive absences because of out-of-school suspensions. Initially, they tried ameliorating this issue by administering in-school suspensions (ISS) instead of out-of-school suspensions (OSS). On paper, this helped lower the number of absences due to OSS. Students serving ISS weren't absent as much. However, the following issues arose from this initial solution.

- Teachers and administrators weren't sure what students should do during ISS.
- Some students saw ISS as a way to get out of class but still not be at home.

As a result, the superintendent implemented what he called the Peace Program. As part of the Peace Program, he created a space in one of his buildings called the Peace Room. Additionally, the school board let him hire a staff member dedicated to monitoring and supervising the Peace Room every day. In addition to having a dedicated staff member to monitor and supervise the room, he adopted and implemented a problem-solving and character-building curriculum for students serving ISS in the Peace Room.

Thus, whenever students served ISS in the Peace Room, they received instruction in problem solving and character building. Plus, this discipline became less of a reward for students because there were now expectations and assignments. Clearly, creating a Peace Room with a designated staff member may not always be an option for schools. That said, this is a good example of how schools and districts can get creative with their staffing.

To onboard staff quickly and efficiently, educators can provide the following.

- **Condensed and video overviews during initial teacher training:** Provide concise but comprehensive training sessions for new staff. These sessions should cover the core principles of restorative practices, the role of responsive circles in the school, and their importance in building positive school culture and maintaining healthy relationships. Focus on practical techniques, such as the responsive circle process detailed in this book.

- **Mentorship and peer observation:** Pair new staff with experienced staff who regularly use restorative practices. The mentor can offer advice, answer questions, and demonstrate how to integrate responsive circles into daily routines. Encourage new staff to observe a few responsive circles in action. This helps them learn the structure, the language, and the process.
- **Resources:** Create a starter tool kit that includes circle prompts, a list of restorative questions or scripts, and an outline of the responsive circle process.
- **Model circles in staff meetings:** Incorporate responsive circles into regular staff meetings. This serves a dual purpose: it models the practice and builds a culture where restorative approaches are not just for students but are part of the entire school community.
- **Ongoing professional learning:** Many districts hire instructional coaches. Have the coaches come and support teachers as they learn about and implement responsive circles.

Funding and Training

In most schools and districts, there are a plethora of competing priorities when it comes to funding. Leaders in charge of school or district budgets try to balance a wide array of needs, all while being good stewards of the coin. There are always academic programs, extracurriculars, and technology integration that must be sufficiently funded. This may not leave much left for initiatives like responsive circles, as they require funding for training, materials, and supplies for items such as talking pieces, reflection journals, data collection tools for monitoring and evaluation, and additional staff if possible.

If you're lucky enough to find staff, those new staff members must be trained. Depending on the training a school or district chooses, that training could be pretty expensive. Districts may be able to offset some of these costs by having training provided by district coaches. These coaches could engage in a train-the-trainer approach, where they receive the initial training and then train teachers back at their buildings. Nevertheless, training for initiatives like responsive circles is essential for effective implementation (Rubio, 2018).

When it comes to funding and training, there are things leaders can do to help with implementation. Again, leaders should prioritize and then clearly communicate the purpose of and expectations regarding new initiatives. Then, schools and districts may be able to offset some costs through the acquisition of grants (Fronius et al., 2019). For example, a simple online search of *restorative practices grants for schools* reveals a variety of grant opportunities for those interested in reforming and improving discipline policy and practice. Some grants are specifically designed for and allocated to districts working to implement conflict resolution programs! This is especially helpful in districts where circles are not prioritized but building-level leaders see their value and want to implement them.

Work with your local regional office of education. These organizations are extremely helpful, recommending trainings or even putting districts and schools in touch with local consultants who can provide trainings at a fraction of the cost when compared to large training and professional development organizations.

If entire districts don't prioritize circles, building-level leaders can prioritize them at their sites. But, at the building level, leaders may not be able to make certain staffing decisions. Most times, whether in collaboration with schools or not, staffing decisions are made at the district level and require school board approval. Building leaders may have different priorities. I believe most, if not all, initiatives gain more traction when they're prioritized at the top. That doesn't mean, however, that you can't implement circles at the building level.

Sustained Momentum

Staff turnover makes sustaining initiatives extremely challenging. However, even though school leadership support is essential, so is buy-in from staff, students, and families. Support at the district level is extremely helpful, too, as this kind of support sends a strong message regarding the district's priorities. Buy-in at all these levels is necessary to sustain restorative practices and responsive circles (Klevan, 2021).

Remember, as members come and go, responsive circles can persist and adapt with a sustainability plan. An example of a responsive circle sustainability plan follows.

- **Develop a clear restorative vision:** Schools should articulate a clear, shared vision for restorative practices and responsive circles that extends beyond individual staff members. This vision must be embedded into school policies, behavior expectations, and daily routines so that any new staff or leadership understand responsive circles are an essential part of the school's culture and approach to managing student conflict.

- **Build a core team of restorative champions:** Sustaining initiatives and cultural changes like this requires training a core group of staff, including teachers, administrators, and counselors, to serve as responsive circle leaders. This group helps provide stability through burnout and turnover by continuously mentoring and training new staff. It also helps when students are involved. When students are involved, as both participants and facilitators, they're actively engaged in leading and supporting the initiative. This helps further embed responsive circles in the school's culture.

- **Institutionalize ongoing professional learning:** Offering regular professional development opportunities for all staff ensures responsive circles remain at the forefront, even when there are chained-in personnel. What's more, when schools make restorative practices and responsive circles part of the onboarding process for new staff, it helps sustain the initiative.

- **Create policies around restoration and reparation:** Make restorative practices and responsive circles a part of the formal discipline policy. When these practices are institutionalized, it's easier for new staff to adopt and use them, even when they're unfamiliar with them.

- **Leverage leadership support:** As with all school initiatives, school leadership is paramount in sustaining momentum. Principals and other administrators should model restorative practices in their interactions with students, staff, and the community.
- **Track data and accountability:** Schools should track the use and success of responsive circles. Leaders should find and incorporate ways to measure how circles impact school culture, disciplinary incidents, and student well-being. These data illustrate the value of responsive circles and build support for them with long-term commitment.
- **Engage the community:** Getting families involved helps extend the momentum beyond the school itself. When parents and other guardians and community members buy into an initiative, they become strong advocates for practices that work.

Leaders and Change Agents Supporting Implementation

In addition to the responsive circle process clearly detailed in chapter 3 (page 37) and a road map for navigating some implementation challenges, embrace the following ideas when supporting the implementation of restorative practices and responsive circles.

- **Understand that conflict happens:** As staff members, we don't all agree. It's logical to presume this would be the same for our students, as well. Therefore, conflict is bound to occur. Once we understand and accept that conflict will occur, we're better prepared to address it when it happens.
- **Become trauma-informed:** Trauma-informed educators understand that many of the students in our classrooms and our schools have experienced a lot. We know, as educators, that many of our students have experienced more traumatic events in their short lives than we have as adults.
- **Focus on relationships:** For teachers and administrators, investing time in relationships is paramount; it helps prevent some disagreements. The strategies familiar to most educators are ways to build such relationships—greeting students at the door every morning; showing interest in their lives outside school; establishing clear, fair expectations and implementing those expectations with consistency; modeling empathy and understanding; checking in with students one-to-one as often as possible; and celebrating diversity and inclusion by showing respect and appreciation for diverse backgrounds. To focus on relationships at the building level, administrators should be regularly visiting classrooms; having open-door policies; actively listening to staff and students; building trust by allowing shared decision making and encouraging staff to take on leadership responsibilities; facilitating responsive circles and advisory meetings with students; being involved in school life, during hours and after; and building community partnerships.

- **Move from punitive to proactive approaches:** For example, reinforce positive student behavior. Administrators and teachers who excel at classroom management can help others improve with a focus on de-escalation. Successfully de-escalating small situations prevents them from becoming major issues.
- **Cultivate a comprehensive, schoolwide community:** School leaders must work to cultivate a strong and connected school community by creating an inclusive, collaborative, and supportive environment where all members—students, staff, families, and community partners—feel valued and engaged. In my school, every person in the school is sorted into a house. This includes all students and all staff members, including maintenance and part-time employees. As part of the house system, we gather once a month to engage in problem-solving and character-building activities. This way, we break down traditional barriers associated with age and grade level.
- **Manage through proximity and be visible:** Going through teacher classroom walkthrough documentation, I've found that I always provide new teachers with this same piece of feedback. I recommend to almost every new teacher that they circulate the classroom early and often. I call this "management through proximity." Often times, our proximity to certain students or groups of students can prevent issues from occurring. Obviously, this can be difficult while teaching, but it's not impossible to circulate the classroom frequently. I take the same approach in hallways, circulating early and often. The closer I am to students, the fewer issues crop up. Also, being visible is extremely helpful. After noticing an increase in student bathroom vandalism, I have parked myself right outside those bathrooms during passing periods as students return from lunch and recess. This has dramatically decreased the vandalism.
- **Understand the change process:** Having a general understanding of the change process is helpful. Furthermore, understand that the dynamics of educational change involve loads of different factors, including but not limited to national, regional, local, school-based, classroom-level, and individual factors (Fullan, 2007).
- **Ensure stakeholder involvement:** As mentioned in the fair process framework, involving others in the change process is beneficial for a variety of reasons. It helps in the ideation phase, when the team is brainstorming ideas and suggestions. It helps in the rollout phase, when the leader can delegate responsibilities to members of the leadership team who've been involved throughout the process. And, it helps extend and procure buy-in. Keep in mind that we can't involve everyone. As a result, someone will feel they should have been asked or involved. They may have beneficial knowledge or skills that could help with the process. Record their wisdom and take it into consideration moving forward.

- **Lead with purpose and articulate the purpose:** Whatever the initiative, it helps everyone when a purpose or vision has been defined and when the reasons behind a new initiative have been explained (Fullan, 2007; McLure & Aldridge, 2022; Meyer-Looze, Richards, Brandell, & Margulus, 2019). Sometimes, depending on the initiative, it helps to redraft the school's vision and mission statement. For example, it could help to focus on relationships, reparation, resolution, and reintegration. Just remember, if you are redrafting the school's vision or mission statements, always include other stakeholders.

- **Clearly articulate expectations:** Like researcher and author Brené Brown (2018) says, "Clear is kind." This is absolutely true. Whatever the initiative may be, it's essential for leaders to be clear regarding their expectations. Not only does a lack of clarity hinder the successful implementation of a new initiative, but it also causes mass anxiety. Change is already hard enough. Compounding change with a lack of clarity needlessly exacerbates the issue.

- **Follow a change model and framework:** They serve as valuable guides and tools to navigate change, reduce risks, and increase the likelihood of successful initiative implementation.

Responsive circles offer an invaluable framework for resolving student conflict in a way that maintains relationships, ensures accountability, and fosters learning and growth. By shifting from traditional punishments to meaningful consequences, schools can cultivate environments where students learn to reflect, communicate, and repair harm. As educators, mastering circle facilitation and understanding the diverse tools available for different types of circles help ensure successful facilitation. While resistance and resource constraints are inevitable, prioritizing relationships and restorative practices can transform both individual classrooms and entire school cultures into spaces where students thrive.

Either with your team or on your own, respond to the discussion questions and consider what next steps to take with the following guidance.

DISCUSSION QUESTIONS

Suppose you're a leader of a school building, a department, or a grade level. How have you helped your team overcome the resistance and anxiety that often accompanies change or new initiatives?

Let's say you're the leader of a school in your district's human resources department. Like the districts in the surrounding areas, it's been difficult to fill positions. What are some strategies you would deploy to attract potential candidates to your school or district?

Imagine being a leader of a school or a district. It's come to your attention that a staff member has been complaining about responsive circles. How do you address it and get this staff member on board with the initiative?

NEXT STEPS

Leverage existing resources. Think about your current system, setting, or structure. Within that context, how might you leverage existing school resources to integrate responsive circles? Can you repurpose time and resources already available to help reduce the strain of resource constraints?

Engage district leadership. Gaining the support and commitment of district leadership can help promote and sustain the momentum needed for change or initiative implementation. How could you share your interest and passion with district leadership in a way that encourages them to support responsive circles in your school?

Use data. Think about sources of data that you could use to help support your responsive circle initiative. What are those sources? How would you use them to paint a clear picture for why the school needs responsive circles?

Epilogue

Remember: traditional disciplinary measures such as detentions, suspensions, and expulsions don't reduce recidivism, increase school safety, or help students learn from their mistakes. More than anything else, traditional punishments:

- Exclude students from the school community
- Put students on a path toward future problems
- Avoid addressing the underlying issues causing misbehavior in the first place
- Ignore an opportunity to teach life skills such as empathy

To have safer schools full of students invested in a solid culture and community, we *teach* them how to make better choices. Just as students come to us not knowing academic content, students also come to us not knowing how to make the best behavioral choices. Restorative practices—especially responsive circles—help students learn how to make the kinds of thoughtful, smart choices that improve everyone's lives.

All this is easier said than done, of course. It always is. Whether in school or in the real world, productively addressing conflict can be extremely difficult. Successfully addressing conflict requires lots of time. It requires a lot of work. It requires bravery. It requires courage. There's often a lot of feelings mixed in, and feelings can be hard to navigate or understand. What's more, most people don't have the training or the experience necessary to productively resolve conflicts. It takes experience and repeated practice. The fact that you are reading this is a sign you're ready for the guidance in this book about why it's important to try this method, how to do so, and how to handle issues that can hinder the practice.

Though we may feel scared for our students, their families, staff, and administrators, there is hope for all. There is hope because our students do care. We can help them show it. There is hope because families want what's best for their children. We can help families show it. There is hope because this field is full of professionals who care deeply about the well-being of students. We all work every day to show it. And, I have hope because there's another way. There's another way to address student misbehavior and help students process and even prevent conflict. I believe the best way forward is the structured and systematic responsive circle process I've laid out in this book.

Individuals like you can make a difference in whether students are successful in avoiding punitive disciplinary actions that exclude them and jeopardize their futures. Change starts small, but it catches on. It grows.

You may feel anxious or nervous about beginning this process. If you start with a circle that has an academic focus, the stakes can feel a little lower. Starting with learning circles, specifically fishbowls, can help you (as well as your students and their families) get a feel for the process and what works well (and what doesn't). When you gather for learning circles, your students don't focus on resolving conflicts. When students facilitate their own learning circles (on a text they're studying, for example), there was always less emotion, if any at all. After reading this book, try learning circles first. After you get comfortable with learning circles, try using circles to resolve conflict.

Either with your team or on your own, respond to the discussion questions and consider what next steps to take with the following guidance.

DISCUSSION QUESTIONS

In addition to viewing student conflict as an opportunity to build relationships with students, how else can you motivate yourself or a team member to take the time to help students properly resolve their conflicts?

In addition to the suggestions provided, what are other ways to help staff embrace and use responsive circles? What are some other ways to help your school community embrace and support responsive circles?

NEXT STEPS

Start a book study. If you just finished this book yourself, take the next step by leading a group of staff members through a book study. Read one chapter a week. Meet before school, during lunch, or after school. Ask members of the group to share their thoughts on the current chapter each week.

Plan a family engagement night. Include education about the topic of circles during a family event or plan a family engagement night around restorative practices and responsive circles. What would you call it? When would you host it? Where would you host it? What information would you share with parents? Explain your thoughts to your team or a colleague.

Get everyone on board. How would you onboard new staff when it comes to responsive circles? What kinds of training would you provide? How can you make this practical and efficient for new staff members, many of whom might be overwhelmed after just starting in a new district?

References and Resources

Abrams, Z. (2022). *What neuroscience tells us about the teenage brain: New research now turns an old assumption on its head, as psychologists seek to optimize social contexts and environments for developing minds.* Accessed at www.apa.org/monitor/2022/07/feature-neuroscience-teen-brain on September 17, 2024.

Achilles, G. M., McLaughlin, M. J., & Croninger, R. G. (2007). Sociocultural correlates of disciplinary exclusion among students with emotional, behavioral, and learning disabilities in the SEELS national dataset. *Journal of Emotional and Behavioral Disorders, 15*(1), 33–45.

Adams, A. T. (2000). The status of school discipline and violence. *The Annals of the American Academy of Political and Social Science, 567*(1), 140–156.

Ahmed, H. (2024, February 7). Four years after apologizing for systemic discrimination, PDSB still suspending & expelling Black & Indigenous students at disturbing rates. *The Pointer.* Accessed at https://thepointer.com/article/2024-02-07/four-years-after-apologizing-for-systemic-discrimination-pdsb-still-suspending-expelling-black-indigenous-students-at-disturbing-rates on September 19, 2024.

Alonso, C., & Romero, E. (2017). Problematic technology use in a clinical sample of children and adolescents: Personality and behavioral problems associated. *Actas Españolas de Psiquiatría, 45*(2), 62–70.

Alt, D., Raichel, N., & Naamati-Schneider, L. (2022). Higher education students' reflective journal writing and lifelong learning skills: Insights from an exploratory sequential study. *Frontiers in Psychology, 12.*

Altenmüller, M. S., Kampschulte, L., Verbeek, L., & Gollwitzer, M. (2023). Science communication gets personal: Ambivalent effects of self-disclosure in science communication on trust in science. *Journal of Experimental Psychology: Applied, 29*(4), 793–812.

Álvarez, B. (2020, November 19). School suspensions lead to stark losses in instructional time. *NEA Today News.* Accessed at www.nea.org/nea-today/all-news-articles/school-suspensions-lead-stark-losses-instructional-time# on July 2, 2024.

Ambrose, M., & Gibson, M. (1995, March). Does suspension work? *NEA Today, 13*(7), 39.

American Psychological Association. (n.d.). *Trauma*. Accessed at www.apa.org/topics/trauma on July 2, 2024.

Andreassen, C. S. (2015). Online social network site addiction: A comprehensive review. *Current Addiction Reports, 2*, 175–184.

The Annie E. Casey Foundation. (2024). *Children in poverty in United States*. Accessed at https://datacenter.aecf.org/data/tables/43-children-in-poverty#detailed/1/any/false/2048,1729,37,871,870,573,869,36,868/any/321,322 on August 8, 2024.

Anyon, Y., Gregory, A., Stone, S., Farrar, J., Jenson, J. M., McQueen, J., et al. (2016). Restorative interventions and school discipline sanctions in a large urban school district. *American Educational Research Journal, 53*(6), 1663–1697.

Anyon, Y., Jenson, J. M., Altschul, I., Farrar, J., McQueen, J., Greer, E., et al. (2014). The persistent effect of race and the promise of alternatives to suspension in school discipline outcomes. *Children and Youth Services Review, 44*, 379–386.

Arcia, E. (2006). Achievement and enrollment status of suspended students: Outcomes in a large, multicultural school district. *Education and Urban Society, 38*(3), 359–369.

Atkins, M. S., McKay, M. M., Frazier, S. L., Jakobsons, L. J., Arvanitis, P., Cunningham, T., et al. (2002). Suspensions and detentions in an urban, low-income school: Punishment or reward? *Journal of Abnormal Child Psychology, 30*(4), 361–371.

Audiophil.io. (2023, September 3). *The psychology of sound: How audio affects emotions*. Accessed at https://audiophil.io/the-psychology-of-sound-how-audio-affects-emotions on September 24, 2024.

Augustine, C. H., Engberg, J., Grimm, G. E., Lee, E., Wang, E. L., Christianson, K., et al. (2018, December 27). *Restorative practices help reduce student suspensions*. Accessed at www.rand.org/pubs/research_briefs/RB10051.html on October 22, 2024.

Balfanz, R., Byrnes, V., & Fox, J. (2015). Sent home and put off track: The antecedents, disproportionalities, and consequences of being suspended in the 9th grade. In D. J. Losen (Ed.), *Closing the school discipline gap: Equitable remedies for excessive exclusion* (pp. 17–30). Teachers College Press.

Bambrick-Santoyo, P. (2018). *Leverage leadership 2.0: A practical guide to building exceptional schools*. Jossey-Bass.

Beck, C. (2024, March 19). *The size of the problem activity ideas* [Blog post]. Accessed at www.theottoolbox.com/the-size-of-the-problem-activity-ideas on September 21, 2024.

Bielas, H., Barra, S., Skrivanek, C., Aebi, M., Steinhausen, H.-C., Bessler, C., et al. (2016). The associations of cumulative adverse childhood experiences and irritability with mental disorders in detained male adolescent offenders. *Child and Adolescent Psychiatry and Mental Health, 10*, Article 34.

Blasco, R. L., Cosculluela, C. L., & Robres, A. Q. (2020). Social network addiction and its impact on anxiety level among university students. *Sustainability, 12*(13), Article 5397.

Blaustein, M., Cook, A., Cloitre, M., DeRosa, R., Ford, J., Henderson, M., et al. (2003). *Complex trauma in children and adolescents* [White paper]. National Child Traumatic Stress Network. Accessed at www.nctsn.org/sites/default/files/resources/complex_trauma_in_children_and_adolescents.pdf on July 2, 2024.

Bluehouse, P., & Zion, J. (1996). Hozhooji naat'aanii: The Navajo justice and harmony ceremony. In M. O. Nielsen & R. A. Silverman (Eds.), *Native Americans, crime, and justice* (pp. 181–189). Westview Press.

Borrows, J. (2010). *Canada's Indigenous constitution*. University of Toronto Press.

Bramley, R., Hall, M.-A., Ely, C., & Robin-D'Cruz, C. (n.d.). *Youth diversion evidence and practice briefing: Minimising labelling*. Accessed at https://justiceinnovation.org/sites/default/files/media/documents/2019-09/minimising_labelling_final.pdf on August 11, 2024.

Bremner, J. D., Vermetten, E., Afzal, N., & Vythilingam, M. (2004). Deficits in verbal declarative memory function in women with childhood sexual abuse-related posttraumatic stress disorder. *The Journal of Nervous and Mental Disease, 192*(10), 643–649.

Brobbey, G. (2018). Punishing the vulnerable: Exploring suspension rates for students with learning disabilities. *Intervention in School and Clinic, 53*(4), 216–219.

Brown, B. (2018, October 15). *Clear is kind. Unclear is unkind*. Accessed at https://brenebrown.com/articles/2018/10/15/clear-is-kind-unclear-is-unkind on August 11, 2024.

Brown, H. L. (1999). The Navajo Nation's Peacemaker Division: An integrated, community-based dispute resolution forum. *American Indian Law Review, 24*(2), 297–308.

Brown, T. M. (2007). Lost and turned out: Academic, social, and emotional experiences of students excluded from school. *Urban Education, 42*(5), 432–455.

Buda, G., Lukoševičiūtė, J., Šalčiūnaitė, L., & Šmigelskas, K. (2021). Possible effects of social media use on adolescent health behaviors and perceptions. *Psychological Reports, 124*(3), 1031–1048.

Bull, F. C., Al-Ansari, S. S., Biddle, S., Borodulin, K., Buman, M. P., Cardon, G., et al. (2020). World Health Organization 2020 guidelines on physical activity and sedentary behaviour. *British Journal of Sports Medicine, 54*(24), 1451–1462.

Burr, R., Kemp, J., & Wang, K. (2024, January). *Crime, violence, discipline, and safety in U.S. public schools: Findings from the school survey on crime and safety—2021–2022* (Report No. NCES 2024-043). U.S. Department of Education. Accessed at https://nces.ed.gov/pubs2024/2024043.pdf on September 18, 2024.

Cai, Y., Yang, Y., Ge, Q., & Weng, H. (2023). The interplay between teacher empathy, students' sense of school belonging, and learning achievement. *European Journal of Psychology of Education, 38*, 1167–1183.

Cavanagh, A. J., Aragón, O. R., Chen, X., Couch, B., Durham, M., Bobrownicki, A., et al. (2016). Student buy-in to active learning in a college science course. *CBE Life Science Education, 15*(4).

Center for Responsive Schools. (n.d.). *Important benefits of extracurricular activities*. Accessed at www.crslearn.org/publication/beyond-the-bell/important-benefits-of-extracurricular-activities on September 22, 2024.

Chen, I., & Forbes, C. (2014). Reflective writing and its impact on empathy in medical education: Systematic review. *Journal of Educational Evaluation for Health Professions, 11*.

Costello, B., Wachtel, J., & Wachtel, T. (2019). *The restorative practices handbook: For teachers, disciplinarians and administrators* (2nd ed.). International Institute for Restorative Practices.

Costenbader, V., & Markson, S. (1994). School suspension: A survey of current policies and practices. *NASSP Bulletin, 78*(564), 103–107.

Costenbader, V., & Markson, S. (1998). School suspension: A study with secondary school students. *Journal of School Psychology, 36*(1), 59–82.

Crouch, E., Radcliff, E., Brown, M., & Hung, P. (2019). Exploring the association between parenting stress and a child's exposure to adverse childhood experiences (ACEs). *Children and Youth Services Review, 102*, 186–192.

Darling-Hammond, S. (2023). *Fostering belonging, transforming schools: The impact of restorative practices.* Accessed at https://learningpolicyinstitute.org/product/impact-restorative-practices-report on September 20, 2024.

da Silva, S. S. P., & da Costa Maia, A. (2013). The stability of self-reported adverse experiences in childhood: A longitudinal study on obesity. *Journal of Interpersonal Violence, 28*(10), 1989–2004.

de Brey, C., Musu, L., McFarland, J., Wilkinson-Flicker, S., Diliberti, M., Zhang, A., et al. (2019, February). *Status and trends in the education of racial and ethnic groups 2018* [Report]. National Center for Education Statistics. Accessed at https://nces.ed.gov/pubs2019/2019038.pdf on July 3, 2024.

de Coninck-Smith, N. (1997). A history of school detention, or "the little confinement." In K. Rousmaniere, K. Dehli, & N. de Coninck-Smith (Eds.), *Discipline, moral regulation, and schooling: A social history* (pp. 73–96). Routledge.

Denver, M., Ballou, A., & DeWitt, S. E. (2024). What's in a label? Public use and perceptions of labeling alternatives in criminology. *Justice Quarterly, 41*(6), 763–789.

Deslandes, S. F., & Coutinho, T. (2020). The intensive use of the internet by children and adolescents in the context of COVID-19 and the risks for self-inflicted violence. *Ciência & Saúde Coletiva, 25*(S1), 2479–2486.

Dignity in Schools Campaign. (n.d.). *What is school pushout?* [Fact sheet]. Author. Accessed at https://dignityinschools.org/wp-content/uploads/2017/10/What-Is-School-Pushout.pdf on October 27, 2024.

Diliberti, M. K., & Schwartz, H. L. (2023, February 16). *Educator turnover has markedly increased, but districts have taken actions to boost teacher ranks.* Accessed at www.rand.org/pubs/research_reports/RRA956-14.html on September 13, 2024.

Dinç, E., Wherley, M. S., & Sankey, H. (2024). Student perception of journaling as an assessment for an engagement experience. *Journal of Experiential Education, 47*(3), 484–503.

Down, B., Sullivan, A., Tippett, N., Johnson, B., Manolev, J., & Robinson, J. (2024). What is missing in policy discourses about school exclusions? *Critical Studies in Education*, 494–512.

Duff, R. A. (2001). *Punishment, communication, and community.* Oxford University Press.

DuFour, R., DuFour, R., Eaker, R., & Many, T. (2010). *Learning by doing: A handbook for Professional Learning Communities at Work* (2nd ed.). Solution Tree Press.

DuFour, R., DuFour, R., Eaker, R., Many, T. W., Mattos, M., & Muhammad, A. (2024). *Learning by doing: A handbook for Professional Learning Communities at Work* (4th ed.). Solution Tree Press.

Dupper, D. R. (1998). An alternative to suspension for middle school youths with behavior problems: Findings from a "school survival" group. *Research on Social Work Practice, 8*(3), 354–366.

Dutil, S. (2020). Dismantling the school-to-prison pipeline: A trauma-informed, critical race perspective on school discipline. *Children and Schools, 42*(3), 171–178.

Dwyer, C. (2021, January 26). *How experience can hinder critical thinking* [Blog post]. Accessed at www.psychologytoday.com/intl/blog/thoughts-thinking/202101/how-experience-can-hinder-critical-thinking on January 10, 2025.

EAB. (2023, February 15). *Two new EAB surveys reveal troubling trends in student behavior: Twice as many teachers witness violent classroom incidents today versus pre-pandemic.* Accessed at https://eab.com/about/newsroom/press/two-new-eab-surveys-reveal-troubling-trends-in-student-behavior on September 13, 2024.

Eckerman, C. O., Davis, C. C., & Didow, S. M. (1989). Toddlers' emerging ways of achieving social coordinations with a peer. *Child Development, 60*(2), 440–453.

Ekstrom, R. B., Goertz, M. E., Pollack, J. M., & Rock, D. A. (1986). Who drops out of high school and why? Findings from a national study. *Teachers College Record, 87*(3), 356–373.

Enright, R. (2022, December 22). *How forgiving others helps you to restore your own humanity: A consequence of forgiving others: You improve your own worth and identity* [Blog post]. Accessed at www.psychologytoday.com/us/blog/the-forgiving-life/202210/how-forgiving-others-helps-you-to-restore-your-own-humanity on September 22, 2024.

Epstein, J. L., Sanders, M. G., Sheldon, S. B., Simon, B. S., Clark Salinas, K., Rodriguez Jansorn, N., et al. (2019). *School, family, and community partnerships: Your handbook for action* (4th ed.). Corwin Press.

Evans, K., & Vaandering, D. (2016). *Little book of restorative justice in education: Fostering responsibility, healing, and hope in schools.* Good Books.

Fabelo, T., Thompson, M. D., Plotkin, M., Carmichael, D., Marchbanks, M. P., III, & Booth, E. A. (2011, July). *Breaking schools' rules: A statewide study of how school discipline relates to students' success and juvenile justice involvement.* Council of State Governments Justice Center. Accessed at https://csgjusticecenter.org/wp-content/uploads/2020/01/Breaking_Schools_Rules_Report_Final.pdf on July 2, 2024.

Feinberg, J. (1965). The expressive function of punishment. *The Monist, 49*(3), 397–423.

Felitti, V. J., Anda, R. F., Nordenberg, D., Williamson, D. F., Spitz, A. M., Edwards, V., et al. (1998). Relationship of childhood abuse and household dysfunction to many of the leading causes of death in adults: The adverse childhood experiences (ACE) study. *American Journal of Preventive Medicine, 14*(4), 245–258.

Finn, J. D., & Servoss, T. J. (2014). Misbehavior, suspensions, and security measures in high school: Racial/ethnic and gender differences. *Journal of Applied Research on Children, 5*(2), Article 11.

First Nations Pedagogy Online. (n.d.). *Talking circles.* Accessed at https://firstnationspedagogy.ca/circletalks.html on September 23, 2024.

Fisher, B. W., & Hennessy, E. A. (2016). School resource officers and exclusionary discipline in U.S. high schools: A systematic review and meta-analysis. *Adolescent Research Review, 1,* 217–233.

Flannery, M. E. (2015, January 5). The school-to-prison pipeline: Time to shut it down. *NEA Today News.* Accessed at www.nea.org/advocating-for-change/new-from-nea/school-prison-pipeline-time-shut-it-down on July 2, 2024.

Fronius, T., Darling-Hammond, S., Persson, H., Guckenburg, S., Hurley, N., & Petrosino, A. (2019, March). *Restorative justice in U.S. schools: An updated research review*. WestEd Justice & Prevention Research Center. Accessed at https://files.eric.ed.gov/fulltext/ED595733.pdf on January 10, 2025.

Fullan, M. (2007). *The new meaning of educational change* (4th ed.). Teachers College Press.

Gale, T., & Parker, S. (2014). Navigating change: A typology of student transition in higher education. *Studies in Higher Education, 39*(5), 734–753.

Gilakjani, A. P., & Sabouri, N. B. (2017). Teachers' beliefs in English language teaching and learning: A review of the literature. *English Language Teaching, 10*(4), 78–86.

Gomis-Pomares, A., & Villanueva, L. (2020). The effect of adverse childhood experiences on deviant and altruistic behavior during emerging adulthood. *Psicothema, 32*(1), 33–39.

Gonser, S. (2021, June 11). *The enduring importance of extracurriculars*. Accessed at www.edutopia.org/article/enduring-importance-extracurriculars on September 22, 2024.

González, T. (2015). Socializing schools: Addressing racial disparities in discipline through restorative justice. In D. J. Losen (Ed.), *Closing the school discipline gap: Equitable remedies for excessive exclusion* (pp. 151–165). Teachers College Press.

Gregory, A., Allen, J. P., Mikami, A. Y., Hafen, C. A., & Pianta, R. C. (2013, January 10). *The promise of a teacher professional development program in reducing the racial disparity in classroom exclusionary discipline* [Conference paper presentation]. Closing the School Discipline Gap: Research to Practice conference, Washington, DC, United States.

Gregory, A., Osher, D., Bear, G. G., Jagers, R. J., & Sprague, J. R. (2021). Good intentions are not enough: Centering equity in school discipline reform. *School Psychology Review, 50*(2–3), 206–220.

Gregory, A., Skiba, R. J., & Noguera, P. A. (2010). The achievement gap and the discipline gap: Two sides of the same coin? *Educational Researcher, 39*(1), 59–68.

Groarke, J. M., Groarke, A., Hogan, M. J., Costello, L., & Lynch, D. (2020). Does listening to music regulate negative affect in a stressful situation? Examining the effects of self-selected and researcher-selected music using both silent and active controls. *Applied Psychology: Health and Well-Being, 12*(2), 288–311.

Groarke, J. M., & Hogan, M. J. (2019). Listening to self-chosen music regulates induced negative affect for both younger and older adults. *PLoS One, 14*(6), Article e0218017.

Guest House. (2019, February 20). *How childhood trauma changes brain chemistry, mental health in adulthood*. Accessed at www.theguesthouseocala.com/how-childhood-trauma-changes-brain-chemistry-mental-health-in-adulthood on July 3, 2024.

Gun-Free Schools Act. (1994). 20 U.S.C. §§ 7961–7965.

Gupta, N., & Sampat, S. (2021, July 29). *How teacher expectations empower student learning*. Accessed at www.brookings.edu/articles/how-teacher-expectations-empower-student-learning on July 2, 2024.

Haidt, J. (2024). *The anxious generation: How the great rewiring of childhood is causing an epidemic of mental illness*. Penguin Press.

Hanna, N. (2008). Say what? A critique of expressive retributivism. *Law and Philosophy, 27*(2), 123–150.

Hannigan, J. D., & Hannigan, J. (2024). *Behavior academies: Targeted interventions that work!* Solution Tree Press.

Harste, J. C., & Burke, C. L. (1977). A new hypothesis for reading teacher research: Both the *teaching* and *learning* of reading are theoretically based. In P. D. Pearson (Ed.), *Reading: Theory, research, and practice* (pp. 32–40). National Reading Conference.

Hashmi, S., Vanderwert, R. E., Paine, A. L., & Gerson, S. A. (2022). Doll play prompts social thinking and social talking: Representations of internal state language in the brain. *Developmental Science, 25*(2), Article e13163.

Hattie, J. (2023). *Visible learning: The sequel: A synthesis of over 2,100 meta-analyses relating to achievement.* Routledge.

Hemphill, S. A., Toumbourou, J. W., Herrenkohl, T. I., McMorris, B. J., & Catalano, R. F. (2006). The effect of school suspensions and arrests on subsequent adolescent antisocial behavior in Australia and the United States. *Journal of Adolescent Health, 39*(5), 736–744.

Hierck, T., & Weber, C. (2024). *Positive behaviors start with positive mindsets: Twenty-eight actions to motivate students and boost achievement.* Solution Tree Press.

Hochman, S., & Worner, W. (1987). In-school suspension and group counseling: Helping the at-risk student. *NASSP Bulletin, 71*(501), 93–96.

Hodges, S. D., & Myers, M. W. (2007). Empathy. In R. F. Baumeister & K. D. Vohs (Eds.), *Encyclopedia of social psychology* (pp. 296–298). SAGE.

Holz, N. E., Boecker, R., Hohm, E., Zohsel, K., Buchmann, A. F., Blomeyer, D., et al. (2015). The long-term impact of early life poverty on orbitofrontal cortex volume in adulthood: Results from a prospective study over 25 years. *Neuropsychopharmacology, 40*(4), 996–1004.

Hunt, M. G., Marx, R., Lipson, C., & Young, J. (2018). No more FOMO: Limiting social media decreases loneliness and depression. *Journal of Social and Clinical Psychology, 37*(10), 751–768.

Infantino, J., & Little, E. (2005). Students' perceptions of classroom behaviour problems and the effectiveness of different disciplinary methods. *Educational Psychology, 25*(5), 491–508.

Isenberg, A. (2019, September 23). *3 types of restorative circles* [Blog post]. Accessed at https://blog.esc13.net/3-types-of-restorative-circles on September 21, 2024.

Ivanov, M. (n.d.). *Behavioral communication: Initial study debrief.* Accessed at http://psyresearch.org/behavioralcommunication on July 2, 2024.

Ivanov, M., & Werner, P. D. (2010). Behavioral communication: Individual differences in communication style. *Personality and Individual Differences, 49*(1), 19–23.

Jacob, G., van den Heuvel, M., Jama, N., Moore, A. M., Ford-Jones, L., & Wong, P. D. (2019). Adverse childhood experiences: Basics for the paediatrician. *Paediatrics and Child Health, 24*(1), 30–37.

Jain, S., Bassey, H., Brown, M. A., & Kalra, P. (2014, September). *Restorative justice in Oakland schools: Implementation and impacts.* Oakland Unified School District. Accessed at www.nycourts.gov/ip/justiceforchildren/PDF/RestorativePracticeConf/P4-Davis-RJ_OUSD_Implementation.pdf on July 2, 2024.

Jimenez, M. E., Wade, R., Jr., Lin, Y., Morrow, L. M., & Reichman, N. E. (2016). Adverse experiences in early childhood and kindergarten outcomes. *Pediatrics, 137*(2), Article e20151839.

Jin, M., Ji, L., & Peng, H. (2019). The relationship between cognitive abilities and the decision-making process: The moderating role of self-relevance. *Frontiers in Psychology, 10*, Article 1892.

Kalmakis, K. A., Shafer, M. B., Chandler, G. E., Aponte, E. V., & Roberts, S. J. (2018). Screening for childhood adversity among adult primary care patients. *Journal of the American Association of Nurse Practitioners, 30*(4), 193–200.

Kalpidou, M., Costin, D., & Morris, J. (2011). The relationship between Facebook and the well-being of undergraduate college students. *Cyberpsychology, Behavior, and Social Networking, 14*(4), 183–189.

Kayama, M., Haight, W., Gibson, P. A., & Wilson, R. (2015). Use of criminal justice language in personal narratives of out-of-school suspensions: Black students, caregivers, and educators. *Children and Youth Services Review, 51*, 26–35.

Kellenberger, E. (2022, March 9). *The classroom environment: The effects of lighting, noise, and air quality*. Accessed at www.openmindschool.org/post/the-classroom-environment-the-effects-of-lighting-noise-and-air-quality on October 25, 2024.

Kim, W. C., & Mauborgne, R. (2003, January). Fair process: Managing in the knowledge economy. *Harvard Business Review*. Accessed at https://hbr.org/2003/01/fair-process-managing-in-the-knowledge-economy on July 2, 2024.

Kinser, P. A., Jallo, N., Amstadter, A. B., Thacker, L. R., Jones, E., Moyer, S., et al. (2021). Depression, anxiety, resilience, and coping: The experience of pregnant and new mothers during the first few months of the COVID-19 pandemic. *Journal of Women's Health, 30*(5), 654–664.

Kirk, D. S. (2009). Unraveling the contextual effects on student suspension and juvenile arrest: The independent and interdependent influences of school, neighborhood, and family social controls. *Criminology, 47*(2), 479–520.

Klevan, S. (2021). *Building a positive school climate through restorative practices*. Accessed at https://learningpolicyinstitute.org/product/wce-positive-school-climate-restorative-practices-brief on September 13, 2024.

Kline, D. M. S. (2016). Can restorative practices help to reduce disparities in school discipline data? A review of the literature. *Multicultural Perspectives, 18*(2), 102–197.

Kokkinos, C. M., Panayiotou, G., & Davazoglou, A. M. (2005). Correlates of teacher appraisals of student behaviors. *Psychology in the Schools, 42*(1), 79–89.

Kotter, J. P. (2012). *Leading change*. Harvard Business Review Press.

Kreatsoulas, C., Fleegler, E. W., Kubzansky, L. D., McGorrian, C. M., & Subramanian, S. V. (2019). Young adults and adverse childhood events: A potent measure of cardiovascular risk. *The American Journal of Medicine, 132*(5), 605–613.

Lacoe, J., & Manley, M. (2019, September). *Disproportionality in school discipline: An assessment in Maryland through 2018*. Regional Educational Laboratory Mid-Atlantic. Accessed at https://files.eric.ed.gov/fulltext/ED598820.pdf on July 2, 2024.

LeBourgeois, M. K., Hale, L., Chang, A.-M., Akacem, L. D., Montgomery-Downs, H. E., & Buxton, O. M. (2017). Digital media and sleep in childhood and adolescence. *Pediatrics, 140*(S2), S92–S96.

Lemert, E. M. (1951). *Social pathology: A systematic approach to the theory of sociopathic behavior.* McGraw-Hill.

Leung-Gagné, M., McCombs, J., Scott, C., & Losen, D. J. (2022, September). *Pushed out: Trends and disparities in out-of-school suspension.* Learning Policy Institute. Accessed at https://learningpolicyinstitute.org/media/3885/download?inline&file=CRDC_School_Suspension_REPORT.pdf on July 2, 2024.

Lewis, S. (2009). *Improving school climate: Findings from schools implementing restorative practices* [Report]. International Institute for Restorative Practices Graduate School. Accessed at https://restorativejustice.org.uk/sites/default/files/resources/files/Improving%20school%20climate.pdf on July 2, 2024.

LiCalsi, C., Osher, D., & Bailey, P. (2021, August). *An empirical examination of the effects of suspension and suspension severity on behavioral and academic outcomes.* American Institutes for Research. Accessed at www.air.org/sites/default/files/2021-08/NYC-Suspension-Effects-Behavioral-Academic-Outcomes-August-2021.pdf on July 2, 2024.

Liu, C., & Ma, J. (2020). Social media addiction and burnout: The mediating roles of envy and social media use anxiety. *Current Psychology, 39*(6), 1883–1891.

Liu, J. (2023, January 30). *Disciplinary referrals, teachers, and the sources of racial disciplinary disproportionalities.* Accessed at www.brookings.edu/articles/disciplinary-referrals-teachers-and-the-sources-of-racial-disciplinary-disproportionalities on September 18, 2024.

Liu, Z., Min, Q., Zhai, Q., & Smyth, R. (2016). Self-disclosure in Chinese micro-blogging: A social exchange theory perspective. *Information and Management, 53*(1), 53–63.

Losen, D. J., & Martinez, P. (2020, October). *Lost opportunities: How disparate school discipline continues to drive differences in the opportunity to learn.* Learning Policy Institute. Accessed at https://learningpolicyinstitute.org/media/508/download?inline&file=CRDC_School_Discipline_REPORT.pdf on July 2, 2024.

Loughran, T. A., Brame, R., Fagan, J., Piquero, A. R., Mulvey, E. P., & Schubert, C. A. (2015, August). Studying deterrence among high-risk adolescents. *Juvenile Justice Bulletin.* Accessed at https://ojjdp.ojp.gov/sites/g/files/xyckuh176/files/pubs/248617.pdf on January 13, 2025.

Lown, B. A. (2016). A social neuroscience-informed model for teaching and practising compassion in health care. *Medical Education, 50*(3), 332–342.

Ma, A., Mumphrey, C., & Lurye, S. (2024, August 30). Why Black students are still disciplined at higher rates: Takeaways from AP's report. *CityNews.* Accessed at https://halifax.citynews.ca/2024/08/30/why-black-students-are-still-disciplined-at-higher-rates-takeaways-from-aps-report-2 on September 19, 2024.

Mabale, J. (2023, September 7). *Attention span by age: How it changes over time* [Blog post]. Accessed at www.neeuro.com/blog/attention-span-by-age on September 23, 2024.

Making Caring Common Project. (n.d.). *How to build empathy and strengthen your school community.* Accessed at https://mcc.gse.harvard.edu/resources-for-educators/how-build-empathy-strengthen-school-community on September 21, 2024.

Malvaso, C. G., Delfabbro, P. H., & Day, A. (2019). Adverse childhood experiences in a South Australian sample of young people in detention. *Australian and New Zealand Journal of Criminology, 52*(3), 411–431.

Maniglio, R. (2011). The role of child sexual abuse in the etiology of suicide and non-suicidal self-injury. *Acta Psychiatrica Scandinavica, 124*(1), 30–41.

Marchbanks, M. P., III, Blake, J. J., Smith, D., Seibert, A. L., Carmichael, D., Booth, E. A., et al. (2014). More than a drop in the bucket: The social and economic costs of dropouts and grade retentions associated with exclusionary discipline. *Journal of Applied Research on Children: Informing Policy for Children at Risk, 5*(2), Article 17.

Marshall, D. (2024, January 8). *How the labeling theory in criminology course can help you raise good children.* Accessed at https://medium.com/@davidmarshall056/how-the-labeling-theory-in-criminology-course-can-help-you-raise-good-children-6fe866119ff7 on October 27, 2024.

Marzano, R. J., Waters, T., & McNulty, B. A. (2005). *School leadership that works: From research to results.* ASCD.

McCluskey, G. (2018). Restorative approaches in schools: Current practices, future directions. In J. Deakin, E. Taylor, & A. Kupchik (Eds.), *The Palgrave International handbook of school discipline, surveillance, and social control* (pp. 607–625). Palgrave Macmillan.

McDonald, S., Kingston, D., Bayrampour, H., & Mail, S. T. (2015). Adverse childhood experiences in Alberta, Canada: A population based study. *Medical Research Archives,* (3).

McLure, F. I., & Aldridge, J. M. (2022). A systematic literature review of barriers and supports: Initiating educational change at the system level. *School Leadership and Management, 42*(4), 402–431.

McPherson, T. (1967). Punishment: Definition and justification. *Analysis, 28*(1), 21–27.

Medical University of South Carolina. (n.d.). *Yawning: Why and what could it mean?* Accessed at https://muschealth.org/medical-services/geriatrics-and-aging/healthy-aging/yawning on July 2, 2024.

Mendez, R. (2021, December 17). In Chicago, high school students have their eyes on social justice. *AFSC News.* Accessed at https://afsc.org/news/chicago-high-school-students-have-their-eyes-social-justice on July 2, 2024.

Merrick, M. T., Ford, D. C., Ports, K. A., Guinn, A. S., Chen, J., Klevens, J., et al. (2019). Vital signs: Estimated proportion of adult health problems attributable to adverse childhood experiences and implications for prevention—25 states, 2015–2017. *Morbidity and Mortality Weekly Report, 68*(44), 999–1005.

Meyer-Looze, C., Richards, S., Brandell, S., & Margulus, L. (2019). Implementing the change process for staff and student success: An instructional module. *International Journal of Educational Leadership Preparation, 14*(1), 170–187.

Michelli, N. M., & Keiser, D. L. (Eds.). (2005). *Teacher education for democracy and social justice.* Routledge.

Mills, L. G., Barocas, B., Butters, R. P., & Ariel, B. (2019). A randomized controlled trial of restorative justice-informed treatment for domestic violence crimes. *Nature Human Behavior, 3*(12), 1284–1294.

Milosavljevic, N. (2019). How does light regulate mood and behavioral state? *Clocks and Sleep, 1*(3), 319–331.

MIT Health. (n.d.). *FAQ: Common reactions to traumatic events.* Accessed at https://medical.mit.edu/faqs/mental-health/common-reactions-to-traumatic-events on July 3, 2024.

Mittleman, J. (2018). A downward spiral? Childhood suspension and the path to juvenile arrest. *Sociology of Education, 91*(3), 183–204.

Mogas, J., & Palau, R. (2021). Classroom lighting and its effect on student learning and performance: Towards smarter conditions. In O. Mealha, M. Rehm, & T. Rebedea (Eds.), *Ludic, co-design and tools supporting smart learning ecosystems and smart education* (pp. 3–12). Springer.

Morelli, M., Casagrande, M., & Forte, G. (2022). Decision making: A theoretical review. *Integrative Psychological and Behavioral Science, 56*(3), 609–629.

Morgan, E., Salomon, N., Plotkin, M., & Cohen, R. (2014). *The school discipline consensus report: Strategies from the field to keep students engaged in school and out of the juvenile justice system.* Council of State Governments Justice Center. Accessed at https://safesupportivelearning.ed.gov/sites/default/files/The_School_Discipline_Consensus_Report.pdf on July 3, 2024.

Morgan, P. L., Farkas, G., Hillemeier, M. M., Wang, Y., Mandel, Z., DeJarnett, C., et al. (2019). Are students with disabilities suspended more frequently than otherwise similar students without disabilities? *Journal of School Psychology, 72*, 1–13.

Morin, A. (n.d.). *Understanding behavior as communication: A teacher's guide.* Accessed at www.understood.org/en/articles/understanding-behavior-as-communication-a-teachers-guide on September 14, 2024.

Morris, E. W., & Perry, B. L. (2016). The punishment gap: School suspension and racial disparities in achievement. *Social Problems, 63*(1), 68–86.

Morrow, B. L., & Kanakri, S. M. (2018). The impact of fluorescent and LED lighting on students attitudes and behavior in the classroom. *Advances in Pediatric Research, 5*, 1–12.

National Center on Safe Supportive Learning Environments. (n.d.). *Relationships.* Accessed at https://safesupportivelearning.ed.gov/topic-research/engagement/relationships on August 27, 2024.

Nelsen, J. (1996). *Positive discipline* (Revised ed.). Ballantine Books.

Nelson-Simley, K. (2020, May 6). *How restorative circles can help students tell their stories.* Accessed at https://knslearningsolutions.com/news/how-restorative-circles-can-help-students-tell-their-stories on September 26, 2024.

Nemeroff, C. B. (2016). Paradise lost: The neurobiological and clinical consequences of child abuse and neglect. *Neuron, 89*(5), 892–909.

Nese, R. N. T., Bastable, E., Gion, C., Massar, M., Nese, J. F. T., & McCroskey, C. (2020). Preliminary analysis of an instructional alternative to exclusionary discipline. *Journal of At-Risk Issues, 23*(1), 1–14.

Noltemeyer, A. L., Ward, R. M., & McLoughlin, C. (2015). Relationship between school suspension and student outcomes: A meta-analysis. *School Psychology Review, 44*(2), 224–240.

Novak, A. (2018). The association between experiences of exclusionary discipline and justice system contact: A systematic review. *Aggression and Violent Behavior, 40*, 73–82.

Novak, A., & Krohn, M. (2021). Collateral consequences of school suspension: Examining the 'knifing off' hypothesis. *American Journal of Criminal Justice, 46*(5), 728–747.

Oaten, J. (2024, April 26). *Combating the attention span crisis in our students.* Accessed at https://santamaria.wa.edu.au/decreasing-attention-spans-jennifer-oaten on July 3, 2024.

Office for Civil Rights. (2016, June 7). *2013–2014 civil rights data collection: A first look: Key data highlights on equity and opportunity gaps in our nation's public schools*. U.S. Department of Education. Accessed at www2.ed.gov/about/offices/list/ocr/docs/CRDC2013-14-first-look.pdf on July 3, 2024.

Office for Civil Rights. (2018, April). *2015–16 civil rights data collection: School climate and safety: Data highlights on school climate and safety in our nation's public schools*. U.S. Department of Education. Accessed at www2.ed.gov/about/offices/list/ocr/docs/school-climate-and-safety.pdf on July 3, 2024.

Ortega, L., Lyubansky, M., Nettles, S., & Espelage, D. L. (2016). Outcomes of a restorative circles program in a high school setting. *Psychology of Violence, 6*(3), 459–468. https://doi.org/10.1037/vio0000048

Osher, D., Cantor, P., Berg, J., Steyer, L., & Rose, T. (2020). Drivers of human development: How relationships and context shape learning and development. *Applied Developmental Science, 24*(1), 6–36.

Owens, J., & McLanahan, S. S. (2020). Unpacking the drivers of racial disparities in school suspension and expulsion. *Social Forces, 98*(4), 1548–1577.

Papouli, E. (2019). Diversity dolls: A creative teaching method for encouraging social work students to develop empathy and understanding for vulnerable populations. *Social Work Education, 38*(2), 241–260.

Partners for Prevention. (n.d.). *Replicating the UN multi-country study on men and violence: Understanding why some men use violence against women and how we can prevent it*. Accessed at https://dl.icdst.org/pdfs/files3/b811e8d3135e37761d6dc68d736a7c46.pdf on January 20, 2025.

Patterson, K., Grenny, J., Maxfield, D., McMillan, R., & Switzler, A. (2008). *Influencer: The power to change anything*. McGraw-Hill.

Payne, A. A., & Welch, K. (2022). Transforming school climate and student discipline: The restorative justice promise for peace. In G. Velez & T. Gavrielides (Eds.), *Restorative justice: Promoting peace and wellbeing* (pp. 153–170). Springer.

Perez, S., & Romkema, J. (2022, October 27). *Talking circles: More than a technique* [Blog post]. Accessed at www.globallearningpartners.com/blog/talking-circles-more-than-a-technique on October 2, 2024.

Perry, A. M. (2019, January 17). *Shaming students is keeping schools from teaching them*. Accessed at www.brookings.edu/articles/shaming-students-is-keeping-schools-from-teaching-them on September 17, 2024.

Planty, M., Hussar, W., Snyder, T., Kena, G., KewalRamani, A., Kemp, J., et al. (2009, June). *The condition of education 2009* (Report No. NCES 2009-081). U.S. Department of Education. Accessed at https://nces.ed.gov/pubs2009/2009081.pdf on July 3, 2024.

Pranis, K. (2005). *The little book of circle processes: A new/old approach to peacemaking*. Good Books.

Pulay, A., & Williamson, A. (2019). A case study comparing the influence of LED and fluorescent lighting on early childhood student engagement in a classroom setting. *Learning Environments Research, 22*(1), 13–24.

Quin, D. (2019). Levels of problem behaviours and risk and protective factors in suspended and non-suspended students. *Educational and Developmental Psychologist, 36*(1), 8–15.

Raffaele Mendez, L. M., & Knoff, H. M. (2003). Who gets suspended from school and why: A demographic analysis of schools and disciplinary infractions in a large school district. *Education and Treatment of Children, 26*(1), 30–51.

Rappaport, N., & Minahan, J. (n.d.). *Breaking the behavior code: How teachers can read and respond more effectively to disruptive students*. Accessed at https://childmind.org/article/breaking-behavior-code on July 3, 2024.

Reach and Teach. (2024, August 11). *The benefits of teaching with comic strip creators: Empowering student creativity*. Accessed at www.reachandteach.net/post/the-benefits-of-teaching-with-comic-strip-creators-empowering-student-creativity on September 25, 2024.

The Responsive Counselor. (n.d.). *Restorative practices in elementary schools*. Accessed at https://theresponsivecounselor.com/2020/04/restorative-practices-in-elementary-schools.html on September 23, 2024.

Rice, K. F., & Groves, B. M. (2005). *Hope and healing: A caregiver's guide to helping young children affected by trauma*. Zero to Three Press.

Ross, R. (2006). *Returning to the teachings: Exploring Aboriginal justice*. Penguin Canada.

Rubio, R. (2018). *Effective implementation practices of restorative justice: A qualitative case study* [Doctoral dissertation, University of La Verne]. ProQuest. www.proquest.com/openview/a7b1ba820ceb30df624b3267716b0f3b/1?pq-origsite=gscholar&cbl=18750

Rumberger, R. W., & Losen, D. J. (2016, June 2). *The high cost of harsh discipline and its disparate impact*. Center for Civil Rights Remedies. Accessed at www.civilrightsproject.ucla.edu/resources/projects/center-for-civil-rights-remedies/school-to-prison-folder/federal-reports/the-high-cost-of-harsh-discipline-and-its-disparate-impact/UCLA_HighCost_6-2_948.pdf on July 2, 2024.

Salicetia, F. (2015). Internet addiction disorder (IAD). *Procedia: Social and Behavioral Sciences, 191*, 1372–1376.

Samimi, C., Han, T. M., Navvab, A., Sedivy, J. A., & Anyon, Y. (2023). Restorative practices and exclusionary school discipline: An integrative review. *Contemporary Justice Review, 26*(1), 28–47.

Samuelson, K. W. (2011). Post-traumatic stress disorder and declarative memory functioning: A review. *Dialogues in Clinical Neuroscience, 13*(3), 346–351.

Sarada, P. A. (2016). Comics as a powerful tool to enhance English language usage. *IUP Journal of English Studies, 11*(1), 60–65.

Sautner, B. (2001). Rethinking the effectiveness of suspensions. *Reclaiming Children and Youth, 9*(4), 210–214.

Schreck, C. J., Miller, J. M., & Gibson, C. L. (2003). Trouble in the school yard: A study of the risk factors of victimization at school. *Crime and Delinquency, 49*(3), 460–484.

Scribner, C. F., & Warnick, B. R. (2021). *Spare the rod: Punishment and the moral community of schools*. University of Chicago Press.

Shabazian, A. N. (2015). The significance of location: Patterns of school exclusionary disciplinary practices in public schools. *Journal of School Violence, 14*(3), 273–298.

Shakya, H. B., & Christakis, N. A. (2017). Association of Facebook use with compromised well-being: A longitudinal study. *American Journal of Epidemiology, 185*(3), 203–211.

Sharma, R. (2023, February 1). *Personality test: Your sitting positions reveals these personality traits.* Accessed at www.jagranjosh.com/general-knowledge/personality-test-your-sitting-positions-reveals-these-personality-traits-1655726286-1 on July 3, 2024.

Sherry, S., & Segato, N. (2024, June 26). *Why are teachers at greater risk of burnout?* [Blog post]. Accessed at www.psychologytoday.com/us/blog/psymon-says/202406/why-are-teachers-at-greater-risk-of-burnout on September 8, 2024.

Skiba, R. J. (2013). Reaching a critical juncture for our kids: The need to reassess school-justice practices. *Family Court Review, 51*(3), 380–387.

Skiba, R. J., Horner, R. H., Chung, C.-G., Rausch, M. K., May, S. L., & Tobin, T. (2011). Race is not neutral: A national investigation of African American and Latino disproportionality in school discipline. *School Psychology Review, 40*(1), 85–107.

Skiba, R. J., & Rausch, M. K. (2006). Zero tolerance, suspension, and expulsion: Questions of equity and effectiveness. In C. M. Evertson & C. S. Weinstein (Eds.), *Handbook of classroom management: Research, practice, and contemporary issues* (pp. 1063–1089). Erlbaum.

Smith, D., Fisher, D., & Frey, N. (2015). *Better than carrots or sticks: Restorative practices for positive classroom management.* ASCD.

Smith, D., Ortiz, N. A., Blake, J. J., Marchbanks, M., III, Unni, A., & Peguero, A. A. (2021). Tipping point: Effect of the number of in-school suspensions on academic failure. *Contemporary School Psychology, 25*(4), 466–475.

Song, H., Zmyslinski-Seelig, A., Kim, J., Drent, A., Victor, A., Omori, K., et al. (2014). Does Facebook make you lonely? A meta analysis. *Computers in Human Behavior, 36,* 446–452.

Spaulding, S. A., Irvin, L. K., Horner, R. H., May, S. L., Emeldi, M., Tobin, T. J., et al. (2010). Schoolwide social-behavioral climate, student problem behavior, and related administrative decisions: Empirical patterns from 1,510 schools nationwide. *Journal of Positive Behavior Interventions, 12*(2), 69–85.

Sprenger, M. (2020). *Social emotional learning and the brain: Strategies to help your students thrive.* ASCD.

Strang, H., Sherman, L. W., Mayo-Wilson, E., Woods, D., & Ariel, B. (2013). Restorative justice conferencing (RJC) using face-to-face meetings of offenders and victims: Effects on offender recidivism and victim satisfaction. A systematic review. *Campbell Systematic Reviews, 9*(1), 1–59.

Takeuchi, H., Taki, Y., Asano, K., Asano, M., Sassa, Y., Yokota, S., et al. (2018). Impact of frequency of internet use on development of brain structures and verbal intelligence: Longitudinal analyses. *Human Brain Mapping, 39*(11), 4471–4479.

Takeuchi, H., Taki, Y., Hashizume, H., Asano, K., Asano, M., Sassa, Y., et al. (2016). Impact of videogame play on the brain's microstructural properties: Cross-sectional and longitudinal analyses. *Molecular Psychiatry, 21*(12), 1781–1789.

Thakur, N., Hessler, D., Koita, K., Ye, M., Benson, M., Gilgoff, R., et al. (2020). Pediatrics adverse childhood experiences and related life events screener (PEARLS) and health in a safety-net practice. *Child Abuse and Neglect, 108,* Article 104685.

Thorsborne, M., & Blood, P. (2013). *Implementing restorative practices in schools: A practical guide to transforming school communities.* Kingsley.

Torkington, S. (2024, January 31). *This is how to help young people navigate the opportunities and risks of AI and digital technology.* Accessed at www.weforum.org/agenda/2024/01/ai-digital-children-risks-opportunities on September 15, 2024.

Tsouloupas, C. N., Carson, R. L., Matthews, R., Grawitch, M. J., & Barber, L. K. (2010). Exploring the association between teachers' perceived student misbehaviour and emotional exhaustion: The importance of teacher efficacy beliefs and emotion regulation. *Educational Psychology, 30*(2), 173–189.

Tuff, A. (2023). *Traditional school discipline is harmful for all.* Accessed at www.idra.org/resource-center/traditional-school-discipline-is-harmful-for-all on January 17, 2025.

UK Violence Intervention and Prevention Center. (n.d.). *The four basic styles of communication.* University of Kentucky. Accessed at https://img3.reoveme.com/m/b4ed24f2672f22ef.pdf on July 3, 2024.

UNICEF. (2024). *Responsible innovation in technology for children: Digital technology, play and child well-being.* Accessed at www.unicef.org/innocenti/reports/responsible-innovation-technology-children#download on September 15, 2024.

University of Cambridge. (2021, February 2). Teaching pupils empathy measurably improves their creative abilities. *ScienceDaily.* Accessed at www.sciencedaily.comreleases/2021/02/210202192751.htm on September 13, 2024.

U.S. Department of Education. (2023, November 15). *U.S. education department's Office for Civil Rights releases new civil rights data on students' access to educational opportunities during the pandemic.* Accessed at www.ed.gov/about/news/press-release/us-education-departments-office-civil-rights-releases-new-civil-rights on September 19, 2024.

Valdez, D., Thij, M. T., Bathina, K., Rutter, L. A., & Bollen, J. (2020). Social media insights into US mental health during the COVID-19 pandemic: Longitudinal analysis of Twitter data. *Journal of Medical Internet Research, 22*(12), Article e21418.

van der Kolk, B. A. (1989). The compulsion to repeat the trauma: Re-enactment, revictimization, and masochism. *Psychiatric Clinics of North America, 12*(2), 389–411.

Wald, J., & Losen, D. J. (2003). Defining and redirecting a school-to-prison pipeline. *New Directions for Youth Development,* (99), 9–15.

Walker, P. (2014). *Complex PTSD: From surviving to thriving.* Azure Coyote.

Wallis, P. (2014). *Understanding restorative justice: How empathy can close the gap created by crime.* Policy Press.

Wang, E. L., & Lee, E. (2019). The use of responsive circles in schools: An exploratory study. *Journal of Positive Behavior Interventions, 21*(3), 181–194.

Wang, X. (2023). Exploring positive teacher-student relationships: The synergy of teacher mindfulness and emotional intelligence. *Frontiers in Psychology, 14,* Article 1301786.

Weingarten, R. (2015, November 8). Our school discipline mistake: We should never have imposed zero tolerance policies on kids. *New York Daily News.* Accessed at www.nydailynews.com/opinion/randi-weingarten-school-discipline-mistake-article-1.2426358 on July 3, 2024.

Wettstein, A., Jenni, G., Schneider, S., Kühne, F., Holtforth, M. G., & La Marca, R. (2023). Teachers' perception of aggressive student behavior through the lens of chronic worry and resignation, and its association with psychophysiological stress: An observational study. *Social Psychology of Education, 26*(4), 1181–1200.

Widom, C. S., DuMont, K., & Czaja, S. J. (2007). A prospective investigation of major depressive disorder and comorbidity in abused and neglected children grown up. *Archives of General Psychiatry, 64*(1), 49–56.

Wijaya, E., Suwastini, N., Adnyani, N., & Adnyani, K. (2021). Comic strips for language teaching: The benefits and challenges according to recent research. *ETERNAL, 7*(1), 230–248.

Wiley, S. A., Slocum, L. A., O'Neill, J., & Esbensen, F.-A. (2020). Beyond the breakfast club: Variability in the effects of suspensions by school context. *Youth and Society, 52*(7), 1259–1284.

Williams, C. P. (2023, July 28). *Covid changed student behavior—How are schools responding?* Accessed at www.edutopia.org/article/covid-changed-student-behavior-how-are-schools-responding on September 14, 2024.

Winter, C. (2016, August 25). Spare the rod: Amid evidence zero tolerance doesn't work, schools reverse themselves. *APM Reports*. Accessed at www.apmreports.org/episode/2016/08/25/reforming-school-discipline on July 3, 2024.

Wolf, K. C., & Kupchik, A. (2017). School suspensions and adverse experiences in adulthood. *Justice Quarterly, 34*(3), 407–430.

The Write of Your Life. (n.d.). *What are restorative circles and how to conduct them* [Blog post]. Accessed at https://thewriteofyourlife.org/what-are-restorative-circles on September 21, 2024.

Zehr, H. (2015). *The little book of restorative justice: A bestselling book by one of the founders of the movement* (Revised and updated ed.). Good Books.

Zhang, D., Katsiyannis, A., & Herbst, M. (2004). Disciplinary exclusions in special education: A 4-year analysis. *Behavioral Disorders, 29*(4), 337–347.

Zhang, K., Li, P., Zhao, Y., Griffiths, M. D., Wang, J., & Zhang, M. X. (2023). Effect of social media addiction on executive functioning among young adults: The mediating roles of emotional disturbance and sleep quality. *Psychology Research and Behavior Management, 16*, 1911–1920.

Zhao, N., & Zhou, G. (2020). Social media use and mental health during the COVID-19 pandemic: Moderator role of disaster stressor and mediator role of negative affect. *Applied Psychology: Health and Well-Being, 12*(4), 1019–1038.

Zion, S. D. (2009). Systems, stakeholders, and students: Including students in school reform. *Improving Schools, 12*(2), 131–143.

Zones of Regulation. (n.d.). *Research and the zones of regulation*. Accessed at https://zonesofregulation.com/research on September 21, 2024.

Index

A

accountability and responsive circles, 6
addiction and the impact of technology and social media, 16, 17
adverse childhood experiences (ACEs), 14–15
affective communication, 84–86. *See also* communication
aggressive communicators, 12. *See also* communication
anxiety, 17
assertive communicators, 12. *See also* communication
attention and focus reduction, 16

B

behavior
    about, 10
    adult misperception and biases regarding student behavior, 13
    as communication, 10–12
    discussion questions and next steps, 18–19
    impact of technology and social media on human development and, 16–17
    scenario for, 9
    theories of misbehavior and conflict, 1
    trauma and, 13–15
    types of communication behavior, 12
bias, 13
body language, 11
brain structure
    impact of technology and social media on human development and, 16
    responsibility and brain development, 26
Brown, B., 104

C

centering or mindfulness circles, 72
circle types and tools. *See also* responsive circles
    about, 71–72
    circle facilitation tools, 76–82
    circle language, 82–86
    circle structure, determining, 44
    circle types and structures, 72–75
    discussion questions and next steps, 87
    scenario for, 71
collective commitments
    reproducibles for, 69
    script for, 58
    steps during the responsive circle, 54–56
comic strips, use of, 80–81
communication
    behavior as, 10–12
    for responsive circles, 93–94. *See also* resistance and resource constraints
consequences, defining, 27. *See also* traditional punishments versus consequences
context and responsive circle, 38–39. *See also* responsive circle facilitation
criminal terminology, avoiding, 83

D

debriefing. *See* post-circle debriefing
detention, 2, 27, 28–29, 52
digital addiction, 16
digital circle facilitation, 74–75
discipline gap, 33

documentation tools, 77–79
dolls and figurines, use of, 81

E

educator resistance, 92–93. *See also* resistance and resource constraints
emotional abuse, 14
expressive function, 24
expulsions, 31–32

F

face-to-face interactions, reduction of, 17
families and guardians
    administrator- or teacher-to-family debriefing, 63
    benefits of responsive circles, 96
    communications and, 94
    discipline detours and, 52
    family and community resistance, 93. *See also* resistance and resource constraints
    meeting locations and, 95
    responsive circle facilitation and, 42, 60
    sustaining momentum and, 102
funding and training for responsive circles, 100–101

H

health issues, 16
Herner, T., 2
household dysfunction, 14

I

implementation
    discussion questions and next steps, 109
    implementation resistance, 90–97
    implementation resource constraints, 97–102
    importance of, 107–108
    leaders and change agents supporting implementation, 102–104
important things to remember about student behavior. *See* behavior
in-school suspensions (ISS), 29–31, 52, 99. *See also* out-of-school suspensions (OSS)
introduction
    book audience and organization, 7–8
    misbehavior and conflict in school, 1–3
    responsive circles: history and efficacy, 3–6

J

journals, use of reflection journals, 81–82

L

leaders and change agents supporting implementation, 102–104
learning circles, 72, 79, 108
lighting, use of, 80

M

meetings
    benefits of responsive circles and, 96
    implementation resistance of responsive circles and, 95–96. *See also* resistance and resource constraints
    morning meetings, 72, 98
    post-circle debriefing and, 59
    prior to the responsive circle, 42–43
mental health concerns, 16
mindfulness
    engaging in mindfulness exercises, 51
    proactive circles and, 72
    reproducibles for, 68
morning meetings, 72, 98
music, use of, 80

N

neglect, 14
nonsequential circles, 44, 73, 74. *See also* circle types and tools
nonverbal communication, 11. *See also* communication
norms, 44–45

O

out-of-school suspensions (OSS), 29–31, 52, 99. *See also* in-school suspensions (ISS)

P

participation. *See also* responsive circle facilitation
    analyzing the harm and, 47–48
    collective commitments and, 54–56
    individual meetings prior to the responsive circle and, 39–42
    number of participants, 43
    participation scripts, 40–41
    preventing future harm and, 51–54
    reintegration and, 56–57
    repairing the harm and, 48–51
    student participation and responsive circles, 97
passive communicators, 12. *See also* communication
passive-aggressive communicators, 12. *See also* communication

perceptions, adult misperception and biases regarding student behavior, 13
physical abuse, 14
post-circle debriefing. *See also* responsive circles
   about, 58
   administrator- or teacher-to-family debriefing, 63
   administrator- or teacher-to-student debriefing, 60–62
   administrator facilitator-to-staff debriefing, 58–60
   checking in after a circle, 61
   discussion questions and next steps, 64
   reproducibles for, 65–70
   teacher facilitator-to-staff debriefing, 60
power structures, 6
prevention, 6, 31, 55
prior to the responsive circle. *See also* responsive circle facilitation
   context and, 38–39
   deciding roles, 45–46
   determining circle structure, 44
   families and, 42
   individual meetings and, 39–42
   investigation and, 39
   norms, choosing, 44–45
   participants, number of, 43
   scheduling the meeting, 42
   settings for the meeting, 42
   talking pieces and, 44
proactive circles, 72, 73. *See also* circle types and tools
professional learning and training, 99, 100–101
punitive disciplinary measures. *See also* traditional punishments versus consequences
   current practices and their historical background, 27–28
   defining punishments, 22, 23–26
   detention, 28–29
   expulsions, 31–32
   impact of, 2
   out-of-school (OSS) and in-school suspension (ISS), 29–31
   reflective questions for punishments, 25
   responsive circles and, 5, 103
   revealing how punishments miss the point, 27–34
   unintended consequences of traditional discipline, 32–34

R

racial inequality and unintended consequences of traditional discipline, 32–33
reactive circles, 72, 73. *See also* circle types and tools

reactive perceptions, 13
reflection journals, use of, 81–82
relationships
   leaders and change agents supporting implementation, 102
   responsive circles and, 5
reproducibles for
   collective commitment agreement, 69
   discipline detour, 67
   mindfulness exercises, 68
   responsive circle notes, 66
   responsive circle reflection, 70
   responsive circle steps, 65
resistance and resource constraints
   about, 89–90
   discussion questions and next steps, 105
   educator resistance, 92–93
   family and community resistance, 93
   implementation resistance, 90–97
   implementation resource constraints, 97–102
   leaders and change agents supporting implementation, 102–104
   scenario for, 89
   sustaining momentum, 101–102
responsive circle facilitation
   about, 38
   circle facilitation tools, 76–82
   participation scripts, 40–41
   post-circle debriefing, 58–63
   prior to the responsive circle, 38–46
   scenario for, 37
   steps during the responsive circle, 46–58
responsive circles. *See also* circle types and tools
   about, 3
   circle language, 82–86
   circle structure, determining, 44
   circle types and structures, 72–75
   efficacy of, 4–6
   history of, 3–4
   time for, 97–98
restorative discipline, 4–5
restorative justice, 4, 5
restorative practice, 5
roles in the responsive circle, 45–46

S

school climate and responsive circles, 5
school-to-prison pipeline, 34
self-esteem and self-perception issues, 17

self-inflicted violence, 16
sequential circles, 44, 73, 74. *See also* circle types and tools
sexual abuse, 14
size of the problem strategy, 53–54
sleep disruption, 16
social media, 2, 16–17
social skills, 16
soft skills, 6
sound machines, use of, 80
staffing and responsive circles, 99–100
steps during the responsive circle. *See also* responsive circle facilitation
- about, 46–47
- analyzing harm, 47–48
- collective commitments, 54–56, 58
- preventing future harm, 51–54
- reintegration, 56–57
- repairing the harm, 48–51

storyboarding, use of, 80–81
stress, 17
student participation and responsive circles, 97
students with special needs, 31, 33

T

talking pieces, 44, 76–77
technology, impact of, 2, 16–17
time and timers, 79
time for responsive circles, 97–98
traditional punishments versus consequences. *See also* punitive disciplinary measures
- about, 22–23
- discussion questions and next steps, 35–36
- distinguishing between punishments and consequences, 23–27
- judging your system's efficacy, 23
- revealing how punishments miss the point, 27–34
- scenario for, 21
- unintended consequences of traditional discipline, 32–34

trauma, 13–15, 102

Z

zones of regulation framework, 53

The Trusted Teacher
Erica Battle
Author Erica Battle's IMPACT framework emphasizes key elements of a trusting classroom environment with practices that are intentional, meaningful, practical, authentic, consistent, and foster teamwork. With reflection prompts and checklists, teachers can connect with their students and build impactful relationships.
BKG191

Behavior Academies
Jessica Djabrayan Hannigan and John Hannigan
With its practical behavior intervention method, this book replaces problematic behaviors with essential life skills for school and beyond. Educators can implement effective targeted interventions in 25 minutes or less using eight predefined behavior academies and a process to create their own.
BKF114

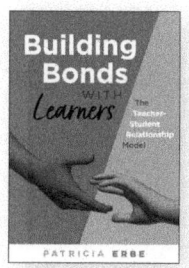

Building Bonds With Learners
Patricia Erbe
Learn to harness the power of relationships and foster a sense of belonging in this research- and experience-based model. K–12 teachers will gain a practical teacher-student relationship methodology for purposefully forming vital connections and lessening academic and behavioral challenges and equity gaps.
BKG170

Embracing Relational Teaching
Anthony R. Reibel
When you shift to relational pedagogy, you establish connections that help students feel valued, respected, and heard, which leads to enhanced student engagement. This book explores the relational approach and offers strategies to embed student-teacher relationships into everyday interactions and learning.
BKF949

Solution Tree | Press
a division of Solution Tree

Visit SolutionTree.com or call 800.733.6786 to order.

Global PD teams
Collaborative Learning for School Improvement

Quality team learning **from authors you trust**

Global PD Teams is the first-ever **online professional development resource designed to support your entire faculty on your learning journey.** This convenient tool offers daily access to videos, mini-courses, eBooks, articles, and more packed with insights and research-backed strategies you can use immediately.

GET STARTED
SolutionTree.com/**GlobalPDTeams**
800.733.6786